Family Recipes

From São Miguel, Azores

M. R. Tiso

Copyright © 2020 by Rita Tiso

All rights reserved.

ISBN 978-1-62806-336-3 (print | paperback)

Library of Congress Control Number 2021919103

Published by Salt Water Media
29 Broad Street, Suite 104
Berlin, MD 21811
www.saltwatermedia.com

Dedication

To my grandmother and mother whose support and lessons from their culinary talents have been my inspiration in this project. Without these two inspirational women, this book could not have been possible. Thank you!

Para a minha Avó e mãe, cujo apaio e talentos culinarias ansinos, me serviran de inspiração pare a realização deste projecto . Sen elas este livro não teria sido possivel. Obrigada!

Introduction

Memories written in our hearts seem almost real. Every detail brings back the magic in the moment; my grandmother, my mother, and I, the wood burning stove in the big kitchen, the long fingers on those skinny hands, never tired of mixing flour and water to make the daily bread.

Those are the same hands that taught me to love and experience particular ways to create the foods that bound us together through the time spent cooking, eating and learning traditions of family.

Many years have passed, but the memories of Avó, (grandmother), and mom still live, thanks to those simple delicious dishes which needed only a few ingredients to create, and a few little tips to become special! Every grand-daughter and grandson has good memories of their beloved grandmother.

We all should look for ways to show love, honor and respect, even if it only means to share recipes done in old fashioned and timeless ways.

Table of Contents

Breads 11
    Flat Bread 13
    Quick and Yeast Bread 27
    Rolls 49

Sweet Breads 57
    Yeast 65

Main Dishes 71
    Beef and Veal 73
    Chicken 81
    Fish 95
    Lamb 127
    Pork 139
    Other Recipes 151

Pancakes 159

Salads 167

Condiments, Relishes, Glazes, Marinades, and Sauces 177

Side Dishes 213

Soups 247

Sweets 271

Butters and Cheese 299

Teas, Flavorings and Other Drinks 315

Tips 319

Recipe Index 329

Breads

Flat Bread, Quick, Yeast, Rolls

Tips for Making Bread

To Knead:

Toss Dough on a floured board or counter. Fold edges of dough toward center, press down and away with palm of hand, turning dough around and around as you knead until it no longer sticks to hand or board. Handle lightly. Dough is ready when smooth and elastic, full of blisters and when pressed with fingers, it springs back.

To Raise Dough:

Grease bowl lightly. Place dough in bowl and turn dough so that all of it is lightly greased. Cover bowl with dish towel. Let rise at room temperature, 70° to 80°F, free from drafts. An unheated oven provides an excellent place. When dough has doubled, punch down, and if time permits, let it rise again. To test if doubled in bulk, poke fingers into the dough. If the dent remains, the dough is ready.

To Shape Loaves:

Roll out dough, roll it up like a jelly roll, pinch ends to seal. Place seam side down in pan. The standard loaf pans are 5 inches x 9 inches or 4 ½ x 8 ½ inches. Do not fill pans more than half full. Cover lightly with towel. Allow dough to rise almost to top of pan.

To Bake:

Bake as directed. To test whether the loaf is done, rap top with knuckles. The loaf should sound hollow. To cool loaves, remove loaves from pans and place on racks until cool. If soft crust is desired, lightly cover loaves during cooling.

Flat Breads

In my grandmothers time, this bread was cooked on a red clay griddle in a wood burning stove.

This recipe was used by most Island families with a variaty of names.

My grandmother called it Bolo de Sertão. My mother called it Short Day Bread. The reason being, she made it when she ran short of bread before she made a new batch of bread for the week. The name stuck, and in Bermuda, my aunt Rose called it Johnny bread.

Growing up, I remember everyone baked the bread. Large families made it twice a week.

Every house had a large brick oven. For us the bread was baked on Saturday. When wood was used for heat, timing was important; time to burn the wood to reach the temperature necessary that was done by sight, depending on the color. When that was done, the ash and left over coals were removed. Next, using a long handled wet mop to the tiles where the loaves of bread were baked. First went in large loaves. On the out side, smaller ones, in the center in front was the roast meat for dinner. When the bread was done, the roast stayed in. Next was the pie or cake for the weekend.

To this day, I love the smell of fresh bread coming out of the oven.

Bolos De Leite
Flat Bread De São Miguel

3 C. Flour
1 C. Sugar
5 oz. Butter
1 tsp. Yeast from instant
2 Eggs
7 oz. milk or as much as needed

Mix flour, sugar and yeast.

Add warm milk with butter and beaten eggs.

Knead dough until it feels elastic and smooth, 10–15 minuutes.

Cover and keep in a draft free warm place. Let it rise until double in size.

Make the dough into small balls the size of an orange.

Sprinkle the bottom of a cookie sheet with flour and place the balls within 1½ inchs apart.

Let it rise again.

Use a cast iron pan, best to flatten each all of dough into a biscuit size.

Cook on medium heat, flip over and cook the other side.

Bolo De Sertão

3 C. all purpose flour
3 tsp. Baking powder
½ tsp. Salt
2 T. sugar
3 T. shortening or lard. I prefer Crisco
1½ to 1¾ cup milk or water

Mix all ingreients together and knead the bread until it feels elastic and smooth.

Form a ball. In a lightly floured board, roll the dough into 1 inch thick.

Preheat griddle, (cast iron frying pan), lightly greased.

Cook on low to medium heat, until golden brown on each side, about 10-12 minutes on each side. It looks similar to a large scone.

Cut into 6 or 8 wedges. Serve with butter, jam or soft cheese.

Note:
My grandmother liked to use half white and half corn flour.

When my son was a teen, he often brought home his friends. One such day, I didn't have many snacks and we know how much teenagers can eat! I thought of my grandmother when grandchildren showed up unexpected, that's what she made.

Pão De Sertão (Tiso Style)

¼ C. sugar
2 C. white flour
2½ T. butter
1 egg
1 C. milk or water
¼ tsp. Salt
2 tsp baking powder
½ C. Parmesean cheese or any other I had on hand.

Mix dry ingredients.

Beat egg with milk or water.

Add to dry ingredients. Mix well.

On a floured pastry board, roll out the dough into a round shape. Flatten to about 1 inch thick.

Cook on a greased iron griddle, low to medium heat, about 8–10 minutes on each side until bread is golden brown.

Cut in wedges and serve with glasses of milk.

Note:
If the frying pan is well seasoned, no need to grease the pan

I double the recipe as one was never enough for growing boys.
Flat bread Tiso style became the most requested snack!

We loved this bread that also became my go to snack for kids. I changed her recipe to suit.

Pita Bread

1 T. active dry yeast
3½ C. all purpose white flour
1¼ C warm water
2 T. olive oil
1 tsp. Salt
½ T. sugar

Combine flour, yeast, sugar, and salt. Make a well in center, add water and oil. Mix into a ball.

On a floured board, work by hand until it forms into a smooth and elastic dough.

Put in a greased bowl in a warm spot, cover with towel, and let rise for 45 minutes.

Punch dough down, divide in to 12 pieces and roll each into a ball.

Let it rest for 10 minutes.

Flatten each ball into a 5 inch circle.

Place on a greased baking sheet, cover and rest for 30 minutes.

Preheat oven to 400° and bake for 9-10 minutes until puffed and lightly browned on bottom.

Immediately wrap in foil and cool.

Saboroso Pão
Savory Focaccia

1 C. warm water
1½ tsp. quick rising yeast
2 tsp. Sugar
⅓ C. extra virgin olive oil, divided
1¾ C. bread flour
1½ tsp. garlic salt
½ C. crumbled feta cheese
⅓ C. chopped pitted olives, any kind
5-6 thin slices of red onions, seperated into rings
1 tsp. dried oregano leaves
1 tsp. Salt.

Use the same process as bread to prepare this dough. Let it rise for 30 minutes.

Coat 15x10x1 inch baking sheet with 1 T. olive oil.

Punch down the dough, knead in feta cheese, olives and oregano.

Cover and let rise until double in size, about 30-45 minutes.

Heat oven to 425°.

Uncover focaccia, dimple surface of dough by pressing with fingertips. Drizzle evenly with 1-2 T. olive oil, sprinkle with salt. Top with onion rings.

Bake 20-25 minutes, or until golden brown.

Bake on bottom shelf of oven at 375°. Be gnerous with oil on pan. Makes a nice crisp bottom.

Beer Bread

3 C. self rising flour
3 T. in sugar
1 (12 oz. can beer)

Combine all ingredients in a bowl and mix well.

Spoon into a greased 9 x 5 x 3 inch loafpan.

Bake at 350° for 50 minutes or until a toothpick inserted in center comes out clean.

Cool 10 minutes in pan; remove to wire rack and cool completely.

Beer bread may be sliced and toasted.

Yeild: One loaf.

Pão De Milho
Corn Bread

3 C. all purpose flour
1½ C. white corn flour (fine) can use Meso
2 T. sugar
1 T. salt
4 T. Crisco
1½ C. boiling water

Stir together the flours, sugar, salt, and Crisco and stir into 1½ C. boiling water until well incorporated. From time to time, stir the dough to cool it.

Mix these ingredients seperately while dough cools.

2-3 T. flour
1½ tsp. sugar
½ C. warm water
1½ tsp. yeast
Stir all together until well incorporated. Set aside to bloom.

(To bloom, means to see small bubbles forming in mixture.)

When dough is comfortable to touch, add the yeast and knead 10 to 15 minutes.

Shape into a ball, and roll into corn flour.

Spray a cookie sheet with pam or coat with Crisco.

Let dough rest for 15-20 minutes. The dough will have cracked.

Bake at 450° for about 1 hour.

Pão De Milho Leve
Corn Light Bread

2 C. cornmeal
1 C. all purpose flour
1 tsp. baking powder
½ C. sugar
1 tsp. Salt.
1 tsp. baking soda
2 C. buttermilk
⅓ C. water
3 T. bacon drippings or oil.

Combine cornmeal, flour, baking powder, sugar, and salt, mixing well.

Dissolve baking soda in buttermilk. Add to cornmeal mixture stirring well.

Add remaining ingredients. Mix well.

Spoon batter into a well greased 8½ x 4½ x 3 inch loaf pan.

Bake at 350° for 1 hour or until golden brown .

Yield: 1 loaf

Pão De Milho Fresco
Fresh Corn Bread

5 ears fresh corn , uncooked
3 eggs, beaten
¾ C. milk
¼ C. plus 1½ tsp. bacon drippings
1½ T. sugar
1 T. baking powder
¾ tsp. Salt
½ C. plus, 1 T. all purpose flour

Cut corn from cob, scraping cob to remove the pulp. Combine corn, eggs, milk, bacon drippings, sugar, baking powder and salt. Stir well.

Gradually stir in flour.

Heat a well greased 8 inch cast iron skillet in a 400° oven for three minutes or until very hot.

Pour batter at 425° for 25 minutes or until golden brown.

Serves 6

Pão De Milho Da Ilha
Island Cornbread

1 C. lard, Crisco or oil
¼ C. sugar
2 eggs
1¾ C. cornmeal
1¼ C. all purpose flour
2 T. baking powder
1 tsp. Salt
1¼ C. milk.

Combine lard, oil or Crisco and sugar, beating well.

Add eggs; beat well

Sift together cornmeal, flour, baking powder and salt.

Add to creamed mixture alternately with milk, beginning and ending with flour mixture.

Spoon batter into a greased 13x9 inch baking pan.

Bake at 450° for 25 minutes or until golden brown.

Pão De Mistura
Mixed Corn Bread

3 C. boiling water
2 C. yellow corn flour, (fine)
3 C. All purpose flour
5 T. buttermilk
1 tsp. Salt
2 T. sugar
1½ C. boiling water

To make yeast:
1 tsp sugar
1½ T. yeast
2 T. all purpose flour
¼ to ½ C. warm water.

Mix corn and white flour with sugar, butter, salt. Bring water to a boil. Let it rest for 10 minutes. Stir well until the flour has taken in all the water adding a little more flour if it seems too wet. Stir from 4-5 times. To speed the dough to rise, return to warm place.

For the yeast, add ¼ to ½ C. warm water, 1 tsp sugar, 1½, T. yeast, 2 to 3 T. flour and beat by hand well - no lumps.

Set aside for the yeast to bloom. You will see small bubbles in dough.

When the dough is at temperature comfortable to the hand, add the yeast and knead. The dough will feel a little wet. That is fine.

Spray dough with Pam. Shape dough into a ball by rolling it into a generous amout of cornmeal. Have a cookie sheet sprayed with Pam. Let dough rise for about 15 minutes. The dough will show cracks when it is ready to bake. Bake at 450° for 1 hour.

Note: Use yellow corn flour, finely ground. Makes 2 loaves.

Pão De Milho Na Sertão
Old Fashioned Skillet Cornbread

6 C. cornmeal
3 C. all purpose flour
1 T. baking powder
1½ tsp. Salt
6 C. milk + 3 T. lemon juice (may replace with buttermilk)
¼ C. plus 2 T. Crisco or mayonaise
3 eggs beaten

Combine cornmeal, flour, baking powder, and salt in a large mixing bowl; mix well, add buttermilk, mayo, and eggs, mixing well.

Heat three well-greased 9-inch cast iron skillets in a 400° oven for 3 minutes or until very hot.

Divide batter among three skillets.

Bake at 425° for 25 minutes or until golden brown.

Yeild: 25 to 30 servings

My grandmother used lard and a large clay pan over a wood burning stove. Mother used Crisco and cast iron on the stove. I changed to mayo because at the time, I didn't have Crisco. The same with the buttermilk. I like it better. For me, using the oven is faster and I can do it all at once.

Pão De Milho Especial
Special Cornbread

1 C. cornmeal
¼ C. all purpose flour
2 tsp. baking powder
¼ tsp baking soda
3 tsp. sugar
1 tsp. Salt
2 eggs
3 T. melted butter
1½ C. milk.

Combine dry ingredients; add the wet ingredients. Mix well.

Heat a well greased 9-inch cast iron skillet in a 400° oven for 3 minutes or until very hot.

Pour batter into hot skillet.

Bake at 400° for 30 minutes.

Yield: 6-8 servings

If any bread is left the next day, cut into 1 inch slices and fry in butter. Serve with sunny side up eggs for breakfast.

Yeast Breads

Memories of baking in a brick oven,

The blazing wood, brilliant flames,

and a primal sense of connection.

Country Bread

1 T. yeast (instant bread machine)
¼ C. Kosher dill pickle juice (can replace with 3 T. vinegar)
1½ C. warm water
1 T. salt
2 T. caraway seeds
1 C. whole wheat flour
3 C. bread flour

Mix flours and yeast, caraway seeds and salt well.

Add the warm water and pickle juice. Mix until flour is blended.

Sprinkle flour on counter or board and knead until smooth.

Cover and let it rise to double in bulk, punch down, and let it rise again, covered.

Pull it into a ball with the seams side down. Let it rise for about 20 minutes.

Bake in a 400° oven for 45 minutes to 55 minutes.

Cheese Bread

1 T. active dry yeast
1½ C. warm milk or water
1 T. sugar
1 T. salt
5½ to 6 C. flour
1½ C. sharp chedder cheese, grated.

Add 1½ C. liquid, sugar, salt and gradually mix. Add yeast in flour Knead dough until smooth.

Let rise until double in bulk.

Punch down dough; knead in cheeses.

Shape into 2 loaves.

Grease pans well.

Bake at 365° for 45 minutes.

Combination Bread

1 T. salt
2 T. sugar
1 C. rolled oats
1 C. corn meal
2 C. boiling water
2 pkgs. Active dry yeast (or 1½ T.)
½ C. lukewarm water
1 C. rye or other flour
1 C. whole wheat flour or use bread flour
1¾ C. white flour

Add salt, sugar, rolled oats and corn meal to the boiling water, stir, and let stand 1 hour.

Add yeast disolved in the ½ C. warm water, then add rye, whole wheat and white flour.

Beat thoroughly, knead about 10 minutes, place in bowl, cover with cloth and let rise.

When doubled in bulk, knead, shape into 2 loaves, cover with cloth let rise in warm place until doubled in bulk.

Bake in a moderately hot oven 375° about 45 minutes.

I prefer to use Fleischmanns Bread machine instant yeast. (1½ T. yeast) Simply add yeast to flour and stir flour, add the warm water to activate yeast.

Dark Bread

⅜ C. corn meal
¾ C. cold water
1 T. Crisco or butter
1 T. Salt
2½ T. caraway seed
1 T. cocoa
1 T. instant coffee
2 packages instant yeast
¼ C. warm water
2 C. rye flour (dark preferably)
1½ C. all purpose flour
1 egg

Add corn meal to ¾ C. boiling water. Remove from heat, stirring constantly until thick.

Stir in shortening, salt, sugar, caraway seeds, cocoa and coffee. Let cool till just warm.

Add yeast to flour and stir. Gradually add flour mixture to warm cornmeal.

When thoroughly mixed, knead on floured board.

Place in greased bowl and punch down. Shape into loaves, place in greased pans, and permit to double.

Shape into loaves, place in pans.

Brush top with egg white.

Bake at 375° for 50 to 60 minutes.

Makes 2 loaves.

Round Herb Loaf

1 pkg. dry yeast
¼ C. warm water
1¼ C. warm milk
3 T. oil
1 egg
2 T. sugar
1½ tsp. Salt
3 C. flour
⅓ C. melted butter
2 T. grated Parmesean cheese
1 T. sesame seeds
½ tsp. garlic salt
½ tsp paprika

Grease a 2 qt. casserole.

Disolve yeast in warm, water. Let stand a few minutes. Add milk, oil, egg, sugar and salt, mixing well. Gradually add flour. Knead briefly on a lightly floured board.

Let rise in warm place until double in bulk

Punch down dough. Pinch off walnut size balls of dough, dip in melted butter. Place in one layer going round the pan.

Mix cheese sesame seed, garlic, salt and paprika. Sprinkle one half of this mixture over the layer of dough, similar to monkey bread.

Proceed in the same manner with the rest of the dough, placing over the bottom layer. Pour remaining butter over dough, sprinkle with the rest of the herb mixture.

Let rise until almost double. Bake at 400° for 25-30 minutes.

Cool in pan for 5-10 minutes. Serve warm.

Pão Caseiro
House Bread

3 C. warm water
3 T. sugar
2 T. yeast
1 T. salt
8 C. flour
cornflour for counter top

Mix water, sugar, salt, and yeast. Stir until disolved.

Add flour and knead by hand or use the Kitchen Aid until dough is smooth, about 5-7 minutes with Kitchen Aid or 10-15 minutes by hand.

Let it rest for 30 minutes.

Fold dough over 8–10 times pulling dough over from sides. We called this giving the bread a hand.

Cover and set aside to rest for about 1 hour, or until double in size.

Sprinkle the counter with corn flour.

Cut the dough in half, fold into a ball, then stretch the dough into a long rectangle. Fold, bringing one long side to center, then the other long side over that. Fold again, this time bringing short end toward center, then bringing other short end over the two layers.

Place dough folded side down into bowl and let rise again, covered.

Flip over onto floured baking sheet. Bake at 350° for 40-50 minutes depending on oven.

Raison Bread Twist

1 pkg. instant dry yeast dissolved in ¼ C. warm water
1¼ C. scalded milk or water
⅓ C. butter
½ C. sugar
1 tsp. Salt
1 egg, beaten
¾ C. raisons
6 C. bread flour
½ tsp. powdered anise (may omit anise)
Poppyseeds, optional

Pour hot milk or water over butter, sugar, and salt in a mixing bowl and when lukewarm, add the yeast and the egg

Mix and knead well on bread board with the rest of the ingredients, using more flour if necessary until smooth and elastic.

Return to bowl. Cover closely and set in a warm place until doubled in bulk.

Form into plain loaves or divide dough into 4 parts. Roll into long strands and with 3 of the strands, make a braid.

Place in a large pan.

Fold the remaining strand double, twist like a rope and lay lengthwise down the center of bread.

Brush with beaten yolk of egg, sprinkle with poppy seed if desired. Let rise until double in bulk.

Bake at 375° for one hour until well-browned.

Makes 1 long loaf or 2 smaller ones.

Pão Rustico
Rustic Bread

3½ C. bread flour
2 tsp. Sugar
½ tsp salt
2 tsp. active dry yeast
1 C. warm water
2 T. extra virgin olive oil
Cooking spray
1 T. cornmeal
1 egg white, beaten

Stir flour, sugar and yeast in a large bowl. Add warm water and oil. Mix well. Turn dough out onto lightly floured surface. Knead until dough is smooth and elastic, about 10 minutes, adding additional flour as necessary.

Coat large bowl with no stick cooking spray. Place dough in bowl, turning to coat top. Cover loosely with plastic wrap or towel.

Let rise in warm place until doubled in size, about 30-40 minutes. Sprinkle baking sheet with cornmeal.

Punch down dough. Shape into oval shaped loaf, about 12 inches long. Place on prepared baking sheet.

Coat loaf lightly with cooking spray. Cover loosely with plastic wrap or towel. Let rise in warm place until double in size, about 30-35 minutes.

Heat oven to 375° and make ½ inch deep lengthwise slash in top of loaf using a serrated knife, or use a razor blade. Brush loaf with egg white. Bake 30-35 minutes or until loaf sounds hollow when lightly tapped.

Makes one loaf.

Sour Dough
(for use in any rye bread)

Reserve 1 C. rye dough previously made. Set in warm place to ferment overnight.

Stir down. Store in refrigerator until needed.

Use ½ C. sour dough instead of a package of yeast in recipe for any rye bread.

Rye Bread (#1)

2 C. light rye flour
2 C. bread flour
¼ C. pickle juice
2 tsp. Kosher salt crushed (don't crush, see below)
2 T. caraway seeds
1¾ C. warm water
2 tsp. white sugar
2 T. active dry yeast.

Mix all dry ingredients. No need to crush salt, add to the warm water to dilute.

Add salted water and pickle juice and stir until incorporated. (May replace with 3 T. vinegar)

Knead on a floured board until smooth and elastic.

Oil the bowl and flip the dough over to be coated, cover and let rise covered with towel, in a draft free place, till double in size.

Punch it down, and form the loaf. Let it rise while the oven is preheating.

Preheat oven to 460° then bake 35–40 minutes.

Remove from pan; let cool on a wire rack.

Rye Bread (#2)

3 C. bread flour
1½ C. rye flour
1 T. salt
1 T. yeast
2 T. trilogy seeds (flax, chia, hemp ... Walmart sells this.)
2 T. sugar

Put all above ingredients in bowl and stir.

Mix 2 C. warm water, 2 T. vinegar or dill pickle juice. Stir into dry ingredients. May need 1 C. more water.

Knead or use bread hook on Kitchen Aid for 7 minutes or by hand for 10-15 minutes.

When done kneading, spray or coat sides of bowl with oil so dough won't stick.

Cover with cloth and put in warm spot for 40 minutes or until doubled in size.

Preheat oven to 460°.

Flour cookie sheet and coat bread with flour.

Score top with razor or serrated kife.

Bake for 45 minutes. Cool on rack.

Rye Bread (#3)

1 package instant dry yeast
¼ C. warm water
½ C. dark corn syrup
1 T. grated orange peel
1½ tsp. salt
2 tsp caraway seeds
2 C. buttermilk
3 C. rye flour
3-3½ C. bread flour

Glaze:
1 T. corn syrup
4 T. water for glaze

Mix syrup, orange peel, salt, caraway seed and buttermilk. Heat until warm. Add to yeast. Gradually add flours.

When all flour has been mixed well into the dough, let rest for 15 minutes before kneading on a floured board.

Place in greased bowl, turning dough so that all sides are greased. Let rise until double in bulk. Punch down and divide into two parts.

Shape each half into a ball. Place on greased baking sheet. Let rise until almost doubled in bulk.

Brush with glaze made of 1 T. corn syrup and 4 T. water.

During the baking, brush twice with same glaze and again immediately after removing from the oven.

Bake at 350° for 45 to 55 minutes and then cool on racks.

Spicy Spiral Loaf

1½ T yeast
2 C. warm milk or water
¼ C. oil
1 T salt
6 C. bread flour

Filling:
1 can (8 oz) black olives
1 (2 oz) jar pimentos
2 T. catsup
2 garlic cloves minced or ¼ tsp garlic powder
½ tsp salt

Add salt, yeast and flour and stir.

To the flour, add water, oil, and when thoroughly blended. Knead well on lightly floured board.

For filling, place all ingredients in the electric blender, or chop olives and pimento very fine. Mix with catsup, garlic and salt. Divide in half.

When dough has doubled in bulk, divide in half. Roll each piece into a rectangle, 4 x 7 inches.

Spread filling over the dough almost to the edge. Roll from long (7") side, being careful to seal edges as you roll. Place seam side down in greased and floured loaf pans.

Brush top with oil and let rise until double in size.

Bake at 400° for 30-40 minutes.

If tops are browning too rapidly, cover pans lightly with foil for the last 15 minutes. Makes 2 loaves.

Basic White Bread

4 C. warm milk, water or combination
4 tsp. Salt
6 T. sugar
¼ C. soft shortening
2 T. active dry yeast
10 C. all purpose white flour

Combine all dry ingredients, add water and warm milk and mix well. May need to add more liquid if dough is too hard or dry.

On a floured boad, work by hand until smooth and elastic dough, about 10 minutes.

Put in a greased bowl. Turn dough over, cover with plastic or towel and let rise in a warm place.

Let rise until double the size.

Punch down and divide into 2 balls for 2 loaves.

Let it rise on cookie sheet or greased, floured loaf pans, about 30-45 minutes.

Preheat oven to 400° and bake for 45-55 minutes or until golden brown. Cover lightly with foil if it browns too quickly.

Remove from oven, let cool on wire rack

White Bread

1 T. dry yeast
2 C. warm water
2 T. shortening
2 T. sugar
1 T. salt
6-6½ C. flour

Pour warm liquid over shortening, salt and sugar. Mix the yeast with half of the flour and beat well.

Add remaining flour gradually. Toss onto a floured counter, and knead until smooth and elastic.

Put dough into greased bowl, cover and let rise until double in size.

Bake at 375° for about 45 minutes.

White Bread (Sponge Method)

1 pkg. Active dry yeast
1 C. warm water
1 tsp. Sugar
2 C. flour
1 C. scalded milk or water
2 tsp. Shortening
1 T. salt
1 T. sugar
4 C. flour

Disolve yeast in 1 C. warm water with 1 tsp. sugar; beat in 2 C. flour to make a smooth batter.

Cover and let rise in a warm place until double in bulk.

To make dough:
Pour the 1 C. scalded milk or water over shortening, salt and 1 T. sugar.

Cool to luke warm. Add to sponge.

Stir in remaining 4 C. flour gradually.

Toss dough on lightly floured board and knead until smooth and elastic.

Place in greased bowl and let rise until double in bulk

Bake at 375° about 45 minutes.

Coffee Sticks

When your basic yeast bread is risen, light and fluffy, cut off small pieces and roll as big as your middle finger, four inches long.

Fold and twist to two inches long and fry in deep oil.

Sprinkle with sugar and cinnamon.

Serve hot with coffee.

Variations To Basic White Bread

Substitute whole wheat or rye flour for one half the bread flour. Cornmeal or oatmeal may be substituted for one third to one half of bread flour.

Whole Wheat Bread (#1)

1 C. warm water
1 C. boiling water
1 T. salt
¼ C. oil
2 C. white flour
4 C. whole wheat flour
2 T. yeast

Add salt and oil to the boiling water. When lukewarm add the mixed white flour, whole wheat flour, and yeast.

Knead until smooth, (add more flour if needed). Let rise in a warm place until doubled in bulk.

Shape into 2 loaves, place in greased and floured pans.

Bake at 350° for 45 minutes until bread shrinks from pan.

For variety, use 2 C. of whole wheat flour and 2 C. of white flour, or 1 C. bran or rye flour with 3 C. of whole wheat flour and 2 C. white flour.

What you want to be sure to have is 4 C. of any combination of flour.

Whole Wheat Bread (#2)

2 C. white flour
2 C. bread flour
2 tsp kosher salt
2 C. warm water
2 T. oil
2 tsp. white sugar
2 tsp active dry yeast.

Mix the dry ingredients excluding salt.

Add salt to warm water and stir. Mix with dry ingredients

On a floured board, knead until smooth and elastic, about 10 minutes.

Oil the bowl, add dough and turn over to coat.

Let it rise to double in size, punch down, shape into a loaf, put in greased, floured pans and cover and let rise for about 30 minutes.

Preheat oven to 460° and bake 34-40 minutes. If the color is not golden browned, remove from pan, return to oven for 5-10 minutes more.

Remove from oven; let cool in a wire rack.

Whole Wheat Bread (#3)

1½ pkgs. yeast
2 C. warm water
2 T. molasses
1 T. salt
3¾ C. whole wheat flour

Dissolve yeast in ½ C. of warm water and stir in molasses.

Add salt to 1½ C. warm water and mix well. Add more water if necessary so that the dough is sticky.

Place in well greased pan. Let rise by about ½ of its volume.

Bake at 450° for 45 minutes.

If a crisper crust is desired, place loaf on oven rack for additional 5 minutes.

Makes 1 loaf.

Whole Wheat Bread (#4)

1 ½ pkgs. Active dry yeast
2 C. warm water
2 T. molasses
1 T. salt
3¾ C. Whole wheat flour

Dissolve yeast in ½ C. of warm water. Stir in molasses.

Add salt, flour and 1 C. of the water. Mix well. Add more water if necessary so that the dough is sticky.

Place in well greased pan. Let rise by about half of its volume.

Bake at 450° for 45-55 minutes.

If a crisper crust is desired, remove loaf from pan, place loaf on oven rack for additional 5 minutes.

Makes 1 loaf.

Rolls

Potato Rolls

2 pkg. Active dry yeast
½ C. Warm water
3½ C. hot milk or water
1 C. mashed potatoes
1 C. of sugar
1 C. of shortening
1 tsp. salt
11 C. of flour

Dissolve yeast in ½ C. of water. Combine next 5 ingredients in a large mixing bowl. Stir until dissolved.

Let stand until lukewarm. Add dissolved yeast.

Stir in enough flour to make a thick batter. Let rise until light.

Mix to a soft dough, adding more flour and beat until smooth and elastic.

Place dough in bowl, then proceed as for other bread recipes as far as kneading.

Shape balls of dough to desired size (suggestion refrigerator rolls) and let rise again in warm place until about double.

Bake at 350° for 30-40 minutes.

Soft Rolls

4 T. butter
2 T. sugar
1 tsp. Salt
2 C. scalded milk
1 pkg. Active dry yeast
¼ C. warm water
1 egg
5½ C. flour

Add butter, sugar and salt to milk. When lukewarm, add yeast disolved in lukewarm water.

Add egg, slightly beaten. Stir in the flour gradually and form into a soft dough. Add only enough more flour to knead. Two large freshly cooked and riced potatoes may be added before the final addition of flour.

Cover and let rise in a warm place until double in bulk.

Toss gently on floured board, handle as little as possible.

Shape according to choice.

Let rise until doubled in bulk.

Bake in a hot oven - 400° for 15-20 minutes until lightly browned.

Remove from oven and brush tops with melted butter.

Use the soft roll dough and make various soft rolls.

Bow Knots

Use soft roll dough recipe.

Pinch off pieces of dough; roll with palm into strips ½ inch thick, 7 inches long.

Tie each strip into a knot.

Let rise until doubled in bulk.

Bake in a hot oven 400° for 15 or 20 minutes until lightly browned.

Remove from oven and brush tops with melted butter.

Braided Rolls

Use soft roll recipe.

Pinch off 3 pieces of dough. Roll with the palm to make each the width of a finger and twice as long. Lay side by side, pinch top ends together and braid loosely.

Press bottom ends together.

Let rise until doubled in bulk.

Bake in a 400° oven for 15-20 minutes until lightly browned.

Remove from oven and brush tops with melted butter.

Clover Leaf Rolls

Use soft roll recipe.

Grease muffin pans. Roll dough into 1 inch balls.

Dip into melted butter. Place 3 in each cup.

Let rise until double in bulk.

Bake in 400° oven for 15-20 minuutes.

Remove from oven and brush tops with melted butter.

Crescent Rolls

Use soft roll recipe.

Roll dough ¼ inch thick in 9 or 10 inch rounds.

Spread with melted butter and cut into pie shaped wedges.

Begin at the wide end roll to point. Draw ends around into crescents.

Let rise until doubled in bulk.

Bake in a 400° oven for 15-20 minutes.

Brush melted butter on top when done.

Mound Rolls

Use soft roll recipe.

Roll dough thin and cut with small biscuit cutter.

Lay two biscuits. One on top of the other in a pan and stand in a warm place to rise.

Brush with sugar and water before placing in oven.

Bake about 20 minutes in a moderately hot 375° oven.

House Rolls

Use soft roll recipe.

Pat dough into a roll, ⅓ inch thick. Cut into rounds 2½ inch across.

Brush well wih melted butter and dip handle of knife in flour and make a crease through the middle.

Press edges together at crease to keep shape.

Place in rows, close together in greased pans.

Let rise until doubled in bulk.

Bake in a 400° oven for 15-20 minutes until lightly browned.

Remove from oven and brush tops with melted butter.

Tea Rolls

1½ tsp. Salt
⅓ tsp. yeast
¼ C. warm water
¾ C. milk
1½ C. flour
¼ C. sugar
1½ tsp. salt
2 eggs
⅓ C. butter
Flour

Add warm water, sugar, milk and salt. Stir to dissolve salt and sugar.

Add beaten eggs and 1½ C. of flour and stir.

Add some flour to knead.

Let rise until doubled in bulk.

Shape into balls - your choice of size or small finger rolls.

Place in buttered pans close together.

When doubled in bulk, bake in 400° oven for 10-20 minutes.

For crusty rolls, set far apart.

If desired, brush tops while hot with ¼ C. confectioners sugar mixed with 2 T. rum.

Pão Doce
Sweet Breads

I love the idea that there are certain foods you don't make in small batches. For example, I don't seem to be able to make just one loaf of sweet bread. Instead, I make double recipes. Use one, and freeze the rest for those days when you need something sweet and have no time to bake.

Pão Doce De Pero
Apple Bread

¾ C. vegetable oil
3 eggs
1 tsp. cinnamon
2 C. sugar
3 C. flour
3 C. finely chopped apples
½ C. chopped nuts
1 tsp. vanilla
1 tsp. salt
1½ tsp. baking soda

Mix all ingredients together.

Pour into 2 greased loaf pans.

Bake at 350° for 1 hour.

Pão De Banana
Banana Bread

¼ C. butter
1¼ C. sugar
2 eggs
1 tsp. Baking soda
4 tsp. Sour cream
2 C. banana pulp mashed
¼ tsp. salt
1 tsp. vanilla
2½ C. flour

Cream sugar and butter; add very lightly beaten eggs.

Add soda dissolved in the sour cream, beat well. Add vanilla and mix.

Pour in a greased and floured pan.

Bake at 350° for 45–60 minutes.

Note: If you are out of sour cream, use equal amounts milk and ¼ tsp. lemon juice.

Pão Doce De Cenoura
Carrot Bread

3 C. flour
2 tsp baking powder
1½ tsp. baking soda
1 tsp. salt
2 tsp. cinnamon
4 eggs
2 C. sugar
10 oz. mashed carrrots
1½ C. vegetable oil
Nuts and raisins to taste.

Beat eggs well with sugar. Combine all ingredients.

Pour batter into 2 loaf pans.

Bake at 350° for 1 to 1½ hours.

Note: Freezes well.

Cranberry Bread

2 C. flour
1 C. sugar
1½ tsp. baking powder
1½ tsp. baking soda
1 tsp. Salt
2 T. grated orange rind
¾ C. orange juice
2 T. melted butter
1 beaten egg
1 C. chopped pecans or walnuts
1 C. chopped raw cranberries

Beat the sugar, juice, butter and egg until smooth.

Add dry ingredients. Beat until incorporated. Fold in the cranberries.

Pour into a greased loaf pan.

Bake at 350° for 60-65 minutes.

Good to have with a cup of coffee or tea.

When in season, buy extra bags of cranberries and keep in the freezer to use during the year.

Poppy Seed Bread

3 C. flour
1 tsp. baking powder
2 C. sugar
1½ tsp. salt
1½ tsp. almond extract
1½ tsp vanilla
1⅛ C. oil
3 eggs
1½ C. milk
2 tsp. poppy seed or more if you like

Combine all ingredients. Beat 2 minutes.

Pour into 2 greased loaf pans.

Bake at 350° for 1 hour, but check at 45 minutes.

Topping:

½ C. sugar
½ tsp almond extract
½ tsp. Vanilla
½ butter extract
¼ C. orange juice

Combine and pour over bread while still hot. Freezes well.

Prune Bread

2 8 oz. pkgs. pitted prunes, chopped
4 C. water
2 C. sugar
¾ C. Crisco or butter
1 tsp. ground cinnamon
1 tsp. ground cloves
½ tsp. salt
2 C. sifted all-purpose white flour
2 tsp. baking soda
2 eggs, beaten

Combine prunes and 4 C. water in a large bowl. Cover and refrigerate overnight.

Drain prunes, reserving 2 C. liquid. Combine prunes, reserved liquid, sugar, crisco, spices, and salt; add eggs.

Sift together flour and soda in a medium mixing bowl.

Add prune mixture to flour mixture, stirring just until dry ingredients are moistened.

Pour batter into 2 greased 9x5x3 loaf pans.

Bake at 350° for 1 hour or until a wooden pick inserted in center comes out clean.

Cool in pans for 10 minutes. Remove from pans and let cool completely on wire racks.

Yield: 2 loaves

Note: At home we used lard, but this must be melted if you use.

Pão Doce De Abobora
Pumpkin Bread

3½ C. all purpose flour
2 C. sugar
2 tsp. baking soda
1½ tsp salt
1 T. ground cinnamon
1 T. ground nutmeg
½ T. ground ginger
1 can pumpkin pie mix, 18 oz.
1 C. vegetable oil
⅔ C. water
4 eggs, slightly beaten

Combine dry ingredients, stir well.

Add pie mix, oil, water, and eggs. Beat 2 minutes at medium speed on electric mixer.

Spoon batter into 2 greased and floured 9x5x3 loafpans.

Bake at 350° for 1 hour and 40 minutes or until a wooden pick inserted in cnter comes out clean.

Cool 10 minutes, remove from pans and cool completely.

Yield: 2 loaves

Sweet Yeast Breads

This bread was traditionaly only made in the Azores Islands.

It was made for all celebrations from Baptisms to weddings to every special event in between.

At Easter, we make the dough into Pombinhas for the children.

I remember hanging around the kitchen waiting with my brothers for the bread to come out of the oven. It is delicious to eat warm with a glass of cold milk.

Pominhas shape is formed fom a rope of dough tied into a knot. It resembles a dove.

For Easter breakfast, we make Flares, using the same dough formed into a small disk about 1 inch thick adding a raw egg in center with two ropes criss crossing the egg and another circling the egg, then baked.

We also made round loaves. Some to give to someone living by themselves or unable to make the bread. I still carry the tradition and so does my son and my daughter in law. "She's making a good Portuguese wife," we say with love, and I quote my son.

They are teaching the children so they too can carry the tradition.

I am writing this book at Easter time, and I am happy to share this tradition with you.

Massa Savada
Sweet Egg Bread

3-4 eggs
1½ sticks butter
2 C. sugar
½ C. of powdered milk
¾ C. water
1 lemon, peel only
4½ C. flour
1½ T. yeast
1 tsp. salt

Cream eggs, butter and sugar until light and fluffy.

In a microwave safe container, add powdered milk and lemon peel to water and bring to a boil. Set aside until warm. Remove lemon peel.

In a bowl, mix flour, yeast, sugar and salt. Add the egg mixture in small amounts to the flour and milk mixture, fully incorporating each addition using the dough hook on a Kitchen Aid or by hand. If by hand, 10 minutes or so.

When all ingredients are incorporated, continue to knead dough until it is soft and smooth. Cover dough and let it rise until doubled in size.

Punch dough and divide into two loaves. Place dough and divide into pans and let it rise until double in size.

Heat oven to 355° - your oven may be different.

Brush top of bread with egg wash. (Egg wash is one egg with a spoon of water beaten together.)

Bake for 45-60 minutes or until done. When kneading the dough, if it feels too hard, add more water.

Massa Doce
Sweet Dough

¾ tsp. Fleischmanns instant dry yeast
1 C. water or milk
4 C. of flour
½ C. softened butter (at room temp.
½ C. sugar
3 eggs
1 tsp. Salt
Grated rind of ½ lemon
3 to 4 C. of all-purpose white flour

Mix salt, yeast and flour.

Cream butter, sugar, and lemon rind. Add one egg at a time, stirring well. After each addition, add milk or water.

Add 3 C. flour a cup at a time and mix

Add the last of the flour, a little at a time as you knead the dough until it is smooth.

Let rise in a warm place until double in bulk.

Cut dough down and form into any desired shape.

Let rise again.

Bake in a 375° oven for 40-55 minutes or until browned, not too dark.

Remember, European pastries tend to be less sweet. If you prefer a little sweeter, adjust the sugar.

Pão Doce Rico
Rich Sweet Dough

¾ T. Fleischmanns instant dry yeast
1½ C. warm milk
1 C. butter.
½ C. sugar
3 eggs
1 tsp. salt
Grated rind of ½ lemon
4-5½ C. flour

Beat butter, sugar, eggs, salt, milk and lemon rind well.

Add the flour and knead until smooth and elastic.

Cover and let rise in a warm place, until double in bulk.

Toss on board and form into any shape.

Let rise in a warm place until double in bulk.

Bake in two loaf pans, or bake shapes on cookie sheets at 375° for 40-55 minutes until browned.

Rich sweet dough does not mean very sweet. With this in mind, you may want to adjust the sugar amount.

Variation

Use the plain sweet dough or the sweet rich dough.

Filling:

¼ C. melted butter
cinnamon and sugar to taste
½ C. golden raisins or more

Roll ½ the recipe of dough ½ inch thick on a floured board. Brush well with melted butter, sprinkle with sugar and cinnamon. Add the raisins.

Begin at one end and roll into a long cylinder.

Place in a well greased long pan or cookie sheet.

Let rise until about doubled in size and bake in a moderate oven, 350° until thoroughly done, about 45 minutes to 1 hour.

Variation 2 (with plums)

Roll the dough flat to ⅓ to 1 inch thick.

Butter a cookie sheet or pan. Transfer dough to the pan.

Spread the filling.

Cut fresh plums in half. Remove the pits place fruit in rows with skins down.

Sprinkle with sugar, Let dough rise for about ½ hour.

Enjoy with a cup of coffee or tea.

Variation 3 (with gingerbread spices)

Roll ½ of the dough to ½ inch thick.

Filling:
¾ C. ground walnuts, (may use more)
½ C. dark brown sugar
½ tsp. ginger
½ tsp. cinnamon
½ tsp allspice
⅓ C. melted buttered
Raw sugar for topping

Mix all ingrediants together.

Spread the dough with the filling.

Roll the dough into a jelly roll and transfer to the pan with the seam down. Brush top with butter and sprinkle with raw sugar.

Bake in a 350° oven for about 35 to 45 minutes.

Main Dishes

Pratos De Veal
Beef Dishes

In the Azores, we have excellent beef dishes. In our family, beef was used for special occasions. I don't know why, but we mostly used fish, chicken and pork. I enjoy a good beef dish, but to this day, I never desire one.

Bovine

In the Azores bovine meat is of excellent quality, produced preominantly on the Islands of Sao Miguel, Terceira and Pico.

This quality comes from the feeding of the animals. The food consists mostly from pastures of good quality grass, grown in the region, throughout the whole year, given the mild climactic conditions that found there.

Baked Beef Stew

½ C. chopped onion
1 clove garlic minced
½ C. olive oil, divided
2 pounds lean beef for stewing cut into 1 inch cubes
½ C. all purpose flour
1 C. tomato juice
2 beef flavored boullion cubes
1 16 oz. can whole tomatoes undrained and chopped
2 C. diced potatoes
1½ C. sliced carrots
½ C. chopped celery
½ C. chili sauce or substitute other hot sauce
½ T. freshly ground black pepper

Saute onion and garlic in 2 T. olive oil in a large skillet until tender. Remove onion and garlic with a slotted spoon and set aside. Reserve drippings in skillet.

Dredge meat in flour and brown in reserved pan drippings over medium heat adding remaining oil as necessary. Set aside.

Bring tomato juice to a boil in a small saucepan. Remove from heat, and add bouillion cubes stirring until disolved.

Combine onion an garlic, carrots, celery, chili sauce, salt and pepper in an oven proof 3 quart casserole. Stir until well blended.

Cover and bake at 325° for 2½ hours, stirring once.

Ladle into individual soup bowls.

Serve hot with corn bread.

Yield 3 quarts.

Meatball Stew

1½ lbs. ground chuck or pork meat ground
¾ C. soft breadcrumbs
1 T. dried minced onion
1¾ tsp. salt divided
¼ C. olive oil
3½ C. water
1 16 oz. can tomato paste
½ tsp. eried whole thyme
2 cloves garlic minced
1 bay leaf
1½ C. cubed potatoes
1 C. sliced celery
1½ C. sliced carrots
2 medium onion, chopped
¼ C. chopped fresh parsley

Combine ground chuck, breadcrumbs, minced oion, ¾ tsp. salt and pepper. Mix well.

Shape mixture into 1½ inch meatballs. Brown in oil in a large skillet over medium heat. Drain off drippings.

Combine meatballs, water, tomato paste, remaining salt, thyme, garlic, and bay leaf. Cover and simmer 30 minutes. Stir in remaining ingredients, cover and simmer 30 minutes, stirring occasionally.

Remove and discard bay leaf.

Serve stew immediately in individual soup bowls.

Yield: 2 qts.

Roast Beef

2½ lbs beef (leg with bone)
4 garlic cloves
1 tsp. cayenne pepper
1 tsp. paprika
3 large onions sliced
8 or 9 oz. chorizo or Italian mild susage or hot to taste.
6 oz. bacon
1 tsp. pepper
2-3 C. of wine (white or red)
1 beer
2 oz. butter

Note: I cover the roasting pan for the first 2 hours.

Remove excess fat from the meat. Crush the garlic into the paprika and cayenne pepper into a paste. Rub the meat well with the paste and rest for 3 hours.

In a clay or enamel baking pan, place a layer of the onions and garlic if any is left from the meat and the chorizo and bacon cut into small bits. Add some peppercorns.

Place the meat on top and pour the wine (on the meat, not in you!) Place in the oven at 350° for 3 hours. As it begins to dry out, add more wine.

From time to time, turn the meat and add a little bit of butter on top of the meat. When meat is half cooked, add the entire beer. Taste, and if needed, add more seasoning.

Allow the flavors to intensify and the sauce to thicken.

Traditionally this is served during the feast of the Holy Spirit.

Rump Roast Beef

4 lbs. rump with bone
¼ lb. bacon
4 T. oil
4 large onions
4 cloves of garlic
1 bay leaf
1 tsp black pepper
1 tsp. of red pepper and salt to taste.
Red wine to taste.

Cut the meat into small pieces. Cut onions into slices.

Add oil and onions to the pot.

Next, add the meat and the rest of ingredients.

Add 1 C. of wine or more if you like.

Cover the pot with the lid, and bake for 2 hours in 325° oven.

After 1 hour, check to see if it needs more wine. You may use more water at this time.

In the olden days, it was made on the fire wood burning oven. This is a very typical dish.

Carne Assada
Roast Beef

Marinate overnight in:
1½ tsp. garlic chopped
1-2 T. pepper relish
1 T. pepper
¾ C. wine (red or white)
¼ C. paprika
salt to taste plus 2 cubes Knorr (beef flavor)
1 C. tomato sauce plain
½ C. olive oil
Root vegetables of choice such as potatoes, carrots, turnips and parsnips.

Gravy:
corn starch
2 egg yolks, beaten
beef broth
1 lemon

Saute in onion in olive oil for 2 minutes. Add 2 cubes knorr and the above. Bring to a boil. Let it cool when cold.

Add beef to the pot. May need a cup of water to barely cover the meat.

The next day:
Cook for 1-2 hours on medium heat. Stir from time to time.

After one hour, test meat for tenderness. When done, remove the meat to a roasting pan.

Add peeled potatoes and or other vegetables into the same pot with the liquid and cook about 15-20 minutes.

With potatoes and other vegetables done, remove to a roasting pan.

In a skillet, add Crisco or oil to about 1½ to 2 inches and fry the potatoes.

Add the meat and fry until golden.

Keep the meat and potatoes in a warm oven until ready to serve.

To finish the gravy, add two beaten egg yolks to the same liquid that cooked the meat and the potatoes.

Add juice of ½–1 lemon and corn starch to thicken. Adjust to taste.

Cream the gravy with the imullsion blender. Bring to a boil and serve with the meat, potatoes and vegetables of your choice.

Note: I like to use some ribs and a less expensive meat, like chuck. Cut the raw chunk of beef into the same size as 2 ribs width as the meat will be cooked a long time, and flavor is better.

I use small yellow potatoes. They don't fall apart.

This roast used to be cooked in the brick ovens.

Chicken

Broiled Bacon Wrapped Chicken

With sweet potatoes and watercress

2 medium sweet potatoes, sliced into ¼ inch thick rounds.
3 T. extra virgin olive oil
coarse salt and freshly ground pepper (to taste)
1 T. packed light brown sugar
2 boneless skinless chicken breast halves (about 12 oz. total each cut into 2 cutlets.)
½ medium red onion, cut into 8 wedges
4 C. watercress (from 1-2 bunches), thick stems removed.
1 T. plus 1 tsp. Champagne or white wine vinegar

Pre-heat broiler with rack 6 inches from heating element.

Place sweet potatoes on a rimmed baking sheet and toss with 2 T. oil. Season with salt and pepper. Spread in a single layer and sprinkle with brown sugar.

Wrap each chicken with bacon, arrange alongside potatoes on sheet, onion, cut side up. Season with salt and pepper.

Broil until chicken is cooked through and potatoes are tender, 8-10 minutes. Toss watercross with remaining 1 T. oil and vinegar and season with salt and pepper. Divide chicken, divide potatoes and watercress evenly among 4 plates and serve.

Chicken a-la King

1 pkg. 10 oz. puff pastry shells
½ C. diced
1 can (10 oz.) cream of chicken soup
½ C. milk
2 C. cubed cooked chicken or turkey
¼ C. diced pimentos.

Bake pastry shells according to pkg. Directions.

In a medium saucepan, cook pepper in butter until tender. Add soup, milk, chicken and pimentos. Heat, stirring occasionally.

Spoon into warm pastry shells. (I buy rather than bake them.)

Makes 6 servings

My grandmother and my mother, made pastry shaped into cups by forming dough over muffin pans upside down, then baked.

Chicken Pot Pie

Filling:
1 T. olive oil
1 T. butter
¼ C. flour
2 C. chicken stock (made from the bone)
2 C. chopped chicken (roasted)
½ C. frozen sweet petite peas
1 large potato diced, and boiled
1½ C. chopped, cooked carrots
½ tsp salt, and cracked pepper to taste
Dash of hot pepper (optional)

Crust:
¾ C. white or yellow cornmeal
¾ C. flour
1 T. baking powder
1½ T. sugar
½ tsp. Salt
¾ cups milk
1 large egg
2 T. canola oil

Pre-heat oven to 400°. Spray the casserole with cooking oil spray.

In a large saucepan, heat olive oil and butter together. Add onion and saute until tender, about 4-5 minutes, add flour, blending slowly. Stir in 2 C. of heated chicken stock, whisking well. Cook mixture over medium heat until thickened and bubbly, about 4 minutes Stir in chicken, peas, potato, carrots, salt, pepper and hot sauce or pepper. Pour into a 2 qt. ovenproof casserole dish coated with cooking spray. Spread mixture evenly. To make crust: In a bowl, stir cornmeal, flour, baking powder, sugar and salt. Stir milk, egg and canola oil until well combined. Stir wet ingredients into dry ingredients. Spoon batter evenly on the filling. Bake at 350° until the top is golden brown, about 20-25 minutes.

Galinha Desfiada Com Legumes
Chicken Pot Pie

6 T. butter
1 medium onion, diced
3 ribs celery, sliced
2 carrots, sliced
1 garlic clove, minced
8 T. flour
1 tsp. Thyme
3 C. chicken broth
3 C. cooked chicken cut into 1 inch cubes
1 C. green beans chopped
1 C. sweet peas
1 C. potatoes peeled and cut into small cubes
1 tsp. salt
½ tsp. pepper
2 eggs, beaten
Puff pastry or pie crust

Preheat oven to 350°. In a large pan, over medium high heat, melt the butter. Add the onion, celery, carrots and garlic.

Cook for about 5 minutes or until the onions are transluscent. Add the flour and thyme and stir for 1 minute. While stirring, gradualy add the rest of the vegetables and chicken broth and bring to a boil. Reduce the heat to medium low, and simmer for 10 minutes. Add salt and pepper, cooking for 2 more minutes.

Divide the filling evenly into 5 (8 oz.) ramekins. Top with puff pastry or pie crust. Make a small X on the top of pastry.

Brush the tops of the pastry with the egg and bake for 30 minutes until the pastry is golden and the filling is bubbling.

Let it rest for 5 minutes. (Note: I use a bag of mixed frozen vegetables.)

Cold Chicken and Pasta

4 or 5 chicken breasts
2 chicken bouillion cubes or 1 T. chicken base.
2½ C. water
¼ C chopped onion
6 oz. Vermicelli (or pasta of your choice)
1 14 oz. can plain artichoke hearts, halved
black olives, optional

Dressing:
1½ T. grated onion
½ C. oil
3 T. red wine vinegar
3 T. lemon juice
1½ T. sugar
1 T. salt
1½ tsp. dried basil, crushed

Dissolve bouillion cubes in water (or use chicken base).

Simmer chicken and onion in bouillion until done, about 45 minutes.

Strain and reserve broth. Remove chicken; allow to cool and chop coarsely.

Break vermicellli into 2 inch pieces. Add enough water to broth to cook pasta according to package instructions.

Dressing: combine all ingredients and mix well.

When pasta is done, drain thoroughly and mix chicken and dressing. Add artichoke hearts and toss.

Refrigerate at least 2 hours or more.

To serve, add tomatos and toss. Add black olives if desired.

Chicken Stew in Bread Bowls

1 5 lb. stewing hen
1 large onion, quartered
1 stalk celery, halved
3 qts. water
¾ pound fresh mushrooms sliced
1 lg. onion, chopped
¼ C. butter
¼ C. flour
¼ C. chopped pimentos
2 tsp. salt
½ tsp. pepper
6 Kaiser rolls or any such type of roll

Combine first 4 ingredients in a large dutch oven. Bring to a boil. Reduce heat, cover and simmer 2 hours. Remove chicken from broth. Let cool slightly. Remove meat from bones, discarding bones. Chop meat into bite size pieces, strain broth, reserve 1 qt.

Discard quartered onion and celery. Reserve remaining broth for use in other recipes. Saute mushrooms and chopped onion in butter in a large dutch oven until tender. Stir in flour. Cook over medium heat 5 minutes, stirring constantly.

Gradually add reserved 1 qt. chicken broth. Cook over medium heat stirring constantly until thickened and bubbly. Stir in reserved chicken, pimento, salt and pepper. Remove from heat . Keep warm.

Cut a slice from top of each kaiser roll to form a lid. Set aside. Remove soft center from each roll and reserve for other uses, leaving shells intact. Place rolls and lids on baking sheet. Bake at 350° for 8 minutes or until lightly browned and crisp. Spoon warm chicken mixture into holes. Place each filled roll and lids on baking sheet.

Serves 6

Chicken Wellington

1 pkg. (17¼) frozen puff pastry sheets
8 small chicken breast cutlets
2 tsp. dried thyme leaves
salt and freshly ground pepper
4 T. butter
1 lg. onion, finely chopped
¼ lb. mushrooms, sliced
1 pkg (3oz) cream cheese
2 T. Dijon mustard
1 or 2 eggs for wash
1 T. butter for sauteing vegetables

Thaw pastry 20 minutes. Sprinkle chicken with seasonings and set aside. Add remaining butter to skillet. Add onion and mushrooms, saute until tender and liquid has evaporated. Stir in parsley. Set aside.

On a lightly floured surface, roll each pastry sheet to 14 inch square, cut into four, 7 inch squares. Combine cream cheese with mustard, spread over chicken cutlets. Spread each pastry square with 2 T. of mushroom mix. Top with chicken breast. Brush edges of pastry with water,seal edges together. Place on parchment paper on ungreased baking sheet. Brush tops with egg wash

Preheat oven to 375°. Bake 25 minutes or until pastry is golden brown.

Makes 8 servings.

Note: I cover the baking sheet with parchment paper.

Writing the Conja de Galinha

Writing the Conja de Galinha recipe, I remember being with my aunts and girl cousins at my grandmothers house. We all sat at the kitchen table.

My cousin Adelide was the first to get married in the family, so the conversation was about the upcoming wedding.

Lunch was ready, Adelide's mother was dishing the food, and my grandmother serving. The dish was conja de galinha. It's made with rice and bits of chicken meat cut into small prices, very similar to risotto.

Adelide was a quiet girl. Advice was given with a good bit of fun.

Grandmother served the guest of honor first, the steam rising from the plate, the aroma permeating the air, reminding me how hungry I was.

Grandmother put plate on the table, then, her hands lovingly on Adelaide's shoulder, said, "Darling, everything will be fine, but don't be too nice on your honeymoon."

Laugher erupted, eating and talking continued. I had no idea as to what that meant.

I was quite young, but I didn't forget much. Later, while learning to cook Conja with grandmother and my mother, I asked grandmother what does it mean."Don't be too nice on your honeymoon, and why shouldn't we be nice all the time?" She smiled and said;

"Sweetheart, when you get married you are young and beautiful. Your husband is so in love with you that eveything your say and do is cute and sexy. That's the time to set your house rules for a happy home."

My grandmother had a way of saying things in a simple way.

Just as her cooking fed our bodies, so did her her loving wise words feed our souls.

Conja De Galinha
Chicken Risotto

Bones of one chicken and wings to make stock
1 C. rice, rinsed 3 times
½ C. onion, chopped fine
2½ T. olive oil and 1½ T. buttered
1 garlic clove mashed
1 or 2 cubes of knorr chicken flavor
salt and pepper to taste
1 T. parsley, chopped
3 celery ribs
½ onion
1 sprig parsley
3 carrots
9 C. water to make stock.

In a pot, add water, chicken bones and wings, knorr, carrots, celery, parsley, salt and pepper. Boil on medium heat for about 45-55 minutes. Let it cool.

Press the broth through a cheesecloth and reserve the broth. From the bones, remove all the bits of meat. Cut into small pieces and reserve.

In a large skillet or dutch oven, add olive oil and onion, saute on medium heat until onion is transluscent. Add garlic and cook for 3 minutes, careful not to burn the garlic. Add rice, cover, with broth.

Keep adding broth, just to cover rice until rice is cooked about 25 minutes or so. At this point, add the meat, salt and pepper to taste and cook for about 3-5 minutes , long enough to warm the meat.

My grandmother always served the conja in soup plates, not in bowls. Sprinkle fresh parsley. Enjoy!

The rice consistancy should be like risotto. This was her recipe.

My mother added one chicken leg for a bit more meat and 1 cup of carrots cut into small cubes.

I like to tell the story how my mother and grandmother fed a family of 5 or 6 for a weekend.

With the chicken broth, a soup is made with veggies and noodles for Saturday night.

Sunday lunch: chicken with potatoes, green vegetable and salad.

Saturday dinner: conja ar resotto.

"That's how you stretch a chicken," my grandmother said.

Sweets were not eaten during the week, but Saturday and Sunday, cake or pie and as we called them, "the good cookies".

During the week, fruits in season and a kind of biscuit, not very sweet, called biscoties.

Serving my dish of conja to grandmother wouldn't be in soup plate, but in a beautiful bowl.

I can hear her now, always with a smile, "Á gente nova, mas a comida e boa, faita á moda de São Miguel."

"Ah! Young people, but the food is good, made Sao Miguel way." She would get up and have a second helping.

My Recipe - Conja De Rita

1 C. rice, rinse 3 times
½ C. onion, chopped fine
1clove garlic mashed
2½ T. olive oil
1½ T. butter
1 T. fresh parsley, chopped
½ C. each, peas, carrots, mushrooms and 2 chicken legs, all chopped into ½ inch pieces
Chicken broth as needed
Juice of ½ lemon

Saute onion until it is almost cooked, not brown. Add garlic and cook 1 or 2 minutes with chicken, carrots and mushrooms.

Add rice and enough broth just to cover, cook on medium to low heat uncovered. Stir often and keep adding broth until the rice is cooked. Add peas 4 minutes before rice is done.

Last, add butter and lemon juice. Serve.

Note: If the lemon is very juicy, 2 tsp. Is enough. Also, I taste the salt content when I buy the broth. Bone broth is the best!

Rosemary Chicken and Brie

1 (8oz) can refrigerated cresent dinner rolls
2 T. finely chopped green onion
6 oz. Brie cheese, rind removed and cubed
1½ C. chopped cooked chicken breast
1 egg beaten
1 tsp. Crushed dried rosemary leaves
1 T. grated parmesan cheese for garnish
1 medium tomato cut into 8 wedges
4 green onions whole, for garnish

Heat oven to 350°. Seperate dough into 4 rectangles.

Spoon ¼ of chopped reen onions onto center of each rectangle. Top with ¼ of cheese cubes. Top with ¼ of chicken, pressing into cheese. Fold pastry into a triangle, seal edges, pierce pastry top.

Place pastry onto ungreased 15x10x1 inch pan. The slashes on top of the pastry allow steam to escape.

Brush with egg. Bake at 350° for 21 to 26 minutes or until golden brown.

Garnish each with tomato wedges and 1 green onion. Let stand 5 minutes before serving.

White Chili

1 T. olive oil
1¼ C. chopped onion
1 C. chicken broth
4 oz. Can chopped green chilies
1 tsp garlic powder
1 tsp. ground cumin
½ tsp oregano leaves
½ tsp cilantro
⅛ to ¼ tsp ground red pepper
1 can 15.5 oz. white beans

In olive oil, saute chicken meat, onion and garlic.

Add all other ingredients except beans, simmer for 30 minutes.

Add beans and simmer for 15 minutes until beans are warm.

Keep it warm for ½ hour to absorb the flavors before serving.

Pratos De Peixe
Fish Dishes

Fish

Seafood is harvested from 1 million square meters, due to the dispersion of the 9 islands, combined with the wealth of its fishing banks.

The many fish are pulled from the seas of the Azores. I will mention some: Boca Negra or (Black Mouth), saurel, grouper, sword fish, sea bream, mackeral, rock fish, sea eel, saw fish, pig fish and, let's not forget, sardines, tuna and chicharro.

Seafood is commonly used daily in most homes.

Bocalhau con Batatos e Cebolas
Cod with Potatoes and Onions

1 large onion sliced and seperated into rings
¾ C. beef bouillion
5 boiled, sliced potatoes
14 oz. cooked cod cut into 1x2 inches
1 T. chopped parsley

In a small saucepan, cook onions in bouillion 4 minutes or until onions are just tender. Drain.

Place ½ of the onion rings, then with ½ of the cod.

Sprinkle with ½ of parsley.

Repeat, slowly pour remaining bouilion over layers.

Bake at 350° for 20 minutes.

Makes 2 servings.

Cod Stew

½ C. onion bouillion
2 T. wine vinegar
¼ tsp curry powder
1 lb. Cod, cut into chunks
½ tsp salt
¼ tsp. pepper
1 small onion cut into wedges seperately

In a skillet, combine bouillion, vinegar and curry powder.

Sprinkle fish with salt and pepper.

Add onions and fish.

Cook covered over moderate heat stirring occasionally for 10 minutes or until fish flakes easily with fork.

Makes 2 servings

Bacalhau a Gomes De Sa
Salt Cod With Potatoes, Onions and Black Olives

1½ lb. salt cod
1 T. plus 1 C. olive oil
6 medium sized potatoes, peeled
4 medium size onions, cut, crosswise into ⅛ inch slices and seperated into rings
½ tsp. finely chopped garlic
18-20 pitted black olives
5 hard cooked eggs, cut crosswise into ¼ inch slices
2 T. finely chopped parsley

Starting a day ahead, place the cod in a bowl. Cover it with cold water and soak for at least 12 hours, changing the water three times.

Pre-heat the oven to 325°.

With a pastry brush, coat the bottom and sides of a casserole 8 inches in diameter and 4 inches deep with 1 T. of olive oil. Drop the potatoes into a pot with enough lightly salted boiling water to cover the potatoes completely. Boil until tender, but not falling apart. Drain, peel and cut the potatoes into ¼ inch slices. Set aside.

Drain the cod, rinse under cold water, place in a saucepan and add enough fresh water to cover the fish by 1 inch. Bring to a boil over high heat. Taste the water. If it seems excessively salty, drain, cover with fresh water, and bring to a boil again.

Reduce the heat to low and simmer uncovered for about 20 minutes, or until the fish flakes easilywhen prodded gently with a fork.

Drain thoroughly. With a small knife, remove and discard any skin and bones and seperate the fish into coarse flakes. Set aside.

In a heavy 10- to 12 inch skillet, heat ½ C. of the olive oil over moderate heat. Add the onion rings, stirring frequently, cook for 5 minutes or until they are soft and transparent, but not brown. Stir in garlic and remove the skillet from heat.

To assemble, spread half the potatoes in the casserole, cover them with half the cod and then half the onions. Repeat the layers with the rest of the potatoes, cod and onions and pour the remaining ½ C. of oil over the top.

Bake in the middle of oven for 20 minutes or until the top is lightly browned. Top with parsley.

Serve the bacalhau from the casserole accompanied by cruets of oil and vinear, and a pepper mill, or dish of freshly ground black pepper.

Creamed Salt Cod

1 lb. Salt cod
2 medium size hot baked potatoes
¾ C. heavy cream scalded
1 C. olive or vegetable oil, warmed
2 cloves garlic, finely chopped
Freshly ground black pepper to taste
Crustless bread triangles, sauted in butter until golden

Cover the salt cod with water and soak 24 hours, changing the water several times.

Drain the cod and cut into four pieces. Place in a skillet with water to cover, bring to a boil, cover and simmer 10 minutes, or until the fish flakes easily. Drain off water and flake fish into the bowl of an electric mixer.

Add the skimmed baked potato to the cod in the mixing bowl. While beating vigorously, gradually add the hot cream, warm oil and garlic until mixture is smooth and thick.

Season to taste with the pepper. Pile the cod mixture in the center of plate, surround with the sauteed bread triangles and serve lukewarm.

Note: In Portuguese cooking a 1,000 plus recipes can be found for cod fish. I chose a few of my favorites.

Serves 8

Salt Cod With Potatoes

1½ lbs. dried salt cod
1 lg. onion, finely chopped (1 C.)
½ C. virgin olive oil or vegetable oil
2 cloves garlic, finely chopped
6 medium size potatoes, cooked and diced
3 T. butter
3 T. flour
1½ C. half and half
Freshy ground pepper to taste
⅛ tsp. ground nutmeg
¼ C. chopped fresh parsley
1 oz. shredded swiss cheese (¼ C.)

Soak the cod in cold water to cover for 24 hours, change the water several times.

In a heavy skillet, saute the onion in the oil over low heat until tender, but not browned. Add the garlic. Cook 2 minutes until tender, but not browned.

Remove the onion and garlic with a slotted spoon to an ovenproof dish.

Flake cod and add to oil remaining in skillet. Add potatoes and cook, stirring 5-7 minutes.

Meanwhile, melt butter in a small saucepan. Blend in the flour and gradually stir in the half and half. Bring to a boil, stirring until bubbly and thick. Add pepper and nutmeg. Pour over cod and potatoes andcook gently, stirring until cod is tender, about 5 minutes. Add parsley and pour over onions. Sprinkle with cheese and glaze and place under a preheated broiler.

Serves 6

Rice With Fish

½ C. olive oil or vegetable oil
2 lg. Onions, finely chopped (2 C.)
2 cloves garlic, finely chopped
2 C. raw long grain rice
1 can (1 lb. 12 oz) tomatoes
4 C. water
¼ C. chopped parsley (flat parsley)
1½ tsp freshly ground pepper
2 lbs. firm white fish fillets such as haddock, halibut, or cod cut into 2 inch chunks
½ lbs. shrimp, shelled and deveined

In a large kettle or dutch oven, heat the oil and saute the onion until tender but not browned. Add the garlic and cook 1 minute.

Add the rice and cook, stirring occasionally until rice is lightly browned. Add tomatos and water from the can. Bring to a boil, cover, and simmer 20 minutes. Add parsley, salt, pepper, fish and shrimp. Push fish down into rice mixture. Cover and simmer 10 minutes, or until fish flakes, shrimp are pink and rice has absorbed liquid.

Serves 8

Everyone knows and likes rice with chicken. This is a cousin that is equally delicious!

Island Baked Bass

1 (2 lb.) dressed bass
¼ C. all purpose flour
¼ C. butter
2 T. half and half
2 C. soft breadcrumbs
½ C. peeled, seeded, chopped tomatoes
½ C. chopped onion
¼ C. peeled, seeded, chopped cucumbers
¼ C. chopped celery
3 T. butter
1 T. chopped celery leaves
½ tsp. salt
¼ tsp. pepper
1½ C. milk

Rinse fish thoroughly. Pat dry, set aside. Conbine flour, ¼ C. butter and half and half, mixing well. Set aside.

Combine bread crumbs, tomato, onion, cucumber, celery, 3 T. melted butter, and chopped celery leaves in a large mixing bowl. Stir mixture well. Sprinkle fish cavity with salt and pepper, and place stuffing in cavity. Close opening with wooden picks and tie with a string.

Place prepared fish in a large shallow roasting pan and spread flour mixture evenly over top. Pour 1½ C. milk around fish.

Bake uncovered at 400° for 45 minutes or until fish flakes easily when tested with a fork. Basting occasionaly with pan drippings, transfer fish to a warm serving platter. Serve immediately.

Yield about 4 servings.

The question is "head on or off?" It's up to you. Also, if you can't get Bass, ask the fish monger for a good substitute for bass. I like to sprinkle a little lemon juice on top of the fish first, before serving.

Fish Cakes

1 C. cold fish shredded
1 C. cold mashed potatoes
1½ T. parsley
1½ T. chives
If using dried, add a little more
1 beaten egg
Flour as needed

Mix fish, potatoes, parsley and chives. Salt and pepper to taste.

Shape into a hamburger-type patty or a ball. Dredge in flour.

Fry in butter unti brown on both sides.

Serve on a bed of crisp lettuce or on a hamburger bun.

Note: A great way to serve leftovers.

Fried Fish with Sauce

3½ lb. fish cut into 3-4 inch pieces
3 large or 4 medium garlic cloves
1 tsp. saffron
1 tsp. paprika
½ tsp of cumin
1 swig of vinegar
Oil to fry as needed
Salt to taste
1 C. water

Clean the fish and sprinkle the fish with salt while the fish is being fried. Peel and firmly chop the carlic, or crush.

Place in a ceramic or glass bowl, adding the saffron, paprika and cumin. Mix well with wooden spoon.

Place the fried fish in the platter where it will be served. At the end, the frying oil is to be removed, leaving a little residue of the fish that was fried.

In a cup of water and garlic, saffron, paprika, cumin, vinegar and salt, mix well and bring to a boil. Be careful when adding the water to the oil in the frying pan. In the frying pan, boiling oil tends to rise.

Serve with boiled potatoes. Toss in parsley butter and salt and pepper.

Broiled Flounder With Mushroom—Wine Sauce

2 lbs flounder fillets
3 T. butter, divided
2 T. lemon juice
1⅛ tsp salt, divided
2 slices bacon, divided
¼ C. chopped green onion
1 small clove garlic finely minced
½ C. sliced fresh mushrooms
1 tsp. all purpose flour
¼ C. catsup
1⅓ C. chable or other dry white wine
¼ C. water

Place fillets in a single layer in a well greased 13x9x2 inch baking dish. Melt 2 T. butter. Pour butter and lemon juice over fillets and sprinkle with 1 tsp. Salt. Broil inches from heating element 10 minutes or until fish, flakes, easily.

Test with fork. Do not turn.

Cook bacon in a heavy skillet until crisp. Drain bacon pieces, reserving drippings in skillet. Add remaining butter to bacon drippings. Saute green onion and garlic in drippings until tender.

Add mushrooms and flour, stirring until smooth. Cook over low heat 1 minute, stirring constantly. Gradually add catsup, wine, water and remaining salt. Cook over medium heat, stirring constantly,until slightly thickened and bubbly.

Place broiled fillets on a serving platter. Spoon sauce over fillets, sprinkle with reserved bacon. Serve immediately.

Yield: 6 servings.

Flounder in the Bag

Parchment paper
¼ lb. fresh mushrooms, sliced
¼ C. plus 2 T. butter, divided
3 T. all purpose flour
1 C. milk
2 T. sherry
½ tsp. salt
¼ tsp. paprika
4 flounder fillets (about 2 lbs.)
½ lb. medium shrimp, peeled and deveined

Cut four 14x12 inch pieces of parchment paper. Cut each into a large heart shape. Fold in half; set aside.

Saute mushrooms in 1 T. butter in a small skillet until tender. Set aside. Melt 3 T. butter in a heavy saucepan over low heat, add flour, stirring until smooth.

Cook 1 minute stirring constantly. Gradually add milk, sherry, and seasonings, cook over medium heat, stirring constantly until mixture is thickened and bubbly.

Stir in sauteed mushooms. Melt remaining butter. Open paper heart out flat and lightly brush surface with butter.

Place 1 flounder fillet on half of each paper heart, top each with one, fourth of shrimp, and pour mushroom sauce evenly over shrimp.

Fold paper edger over to seal securely. Carefully place parchment bags on a baking sheet. Bake at 425° for 15 minutes or until bags are puffed and lightly browned. Place on individual serving plates before cutting and opening in bags.

Yield 4 servings.

Poached Grouper

2 qts. water
1 large onion, quartered
1 tsp. salt
½ tsp pepper
2½ lbs grouper fillets cut into srving size pieces
Fresh parsley sprigs.

Combine water, onion, salt and pepper in a large dutch oven, stirring well. Bring mixture to a boil, add fish, and cook 15 minutes or until fish is done. Remove from heat.

Transfer fish and onion to a serving platter using a slotted spoon.

Garnish plater with parsley sprigs and serve with fish stock, if desired.

Yield 6 servings.

Grilled Salmon Steaks

4 (1inch thick) salmon steaks
½ C. buttered juice of one lemon
½ tsp. salt
¼ tsp white pepper
1½ tsp. fresh dill

Rinse the steaks thoroughly in cold water, drain and pat dry.

Place steaks in a wire grilling basket.

Combine butter, lemon juice, salt and pepper. Stir well.

Grill steaks over medium coals, 10 minutes on each side or until fish flakes easily when tested with a fork. Baste often with butter mixture, reserving a small amout for sauce.

For the sauce, add dill to remaining butter mixture. Stir well.

Serve steaks with dill butter sauce.

Yield: 4 servings

Steamed Salmon

¼ C. water
4 (1 inch thick) salmon steaks
2 T. olive oil
1 onion sliced in rounds
Juice of ½ lemon
½ tsp. salt
½ tsp. pepper (white)
1 tsp fresh dill (or dried 1½ tsp.)

Rinse the salmon thoroughly in cold water. Drain and pat dry.

Place the onion rings, olive oil and a ¼ C. of water in an iron skillet.

Add salmon steaks, sprinkle with salt, pepper, dill and squeeze lemon juice.

Cover skillet and cook for about 8-10 minutes.

Test for doneness. Liquid on bottom of skillet may need a little more cooking. (Don't over cook.)

When salmon is done, remove to a serving platter. Cook onions until golden brown. Add to each serving of salmon.

Yield: 4 servings

Baked Stuffed Red Snapper

1 lb. fresh shrimp, any size, peeled and deveined
1 lg. onion, chopped
2 cloves garlic, minced
1 T. butter, melted
¼ C. water
6 slices bread
Small sweet pepper finely chopped
2 T. chopped fresh parsley
1 T. chopped celery
¾ tsp. salt
¼ tsp pepper
dash of dried whole thyme
8 red snapper fillets (about 4 lbs)
Fresh parsley sprigs, optional

Saute shrimp, onion and garlic in oil in a large skillet about 15 minutes over medium heat.

Sprinkle water over bread. Mash and add to shrimp mixture. Add the other ingredients. Simmer 10 minutes.

Place 4 fillets on a large broiler pan. Evenly spoon one fourth of stuffing mixture on each fillet. Top with reserved fillets, and fasten with wooden picks. Pour sauce over stuffed fillets.

Bake at 350° for 30 minutes or until fillets flake easily when tested with a fork.

Transfer stuffed fillets to a large serving platter. Garnish with fresh parsley sprigs if desired. Finish with Snapper Sauce found in Sauces section.

Note: 1 (5-7 pounds) red snapper may be substituted for fillets.

Yield: 8 servings.

Baked Snapper

½ C. olive oil
4 medium onions chopped
4 cloves garlic, minced
1 C. chopped celery
1 small green pepper chopped
5 medium tomatoes, peeled and quartered
1 C. water
1 tsp. Dried whole oregano
¼ tsp. Salt
1 (2 lb.) dressed snapper
1 T. olive oil
1 T. (calda da pimente) or a pinch of cayenne peppercorns
Watercress for garnish if desired

Combine first 10 ingredients in a large skillet. Cook over medium heat 15 minutes or until vegetables are tender. Rinse fish thoroughly in cold water, pat dry, and place in a greased 13x9x2inch baking pan.

Brush fish with 1 T. olive oil. Spoon vegetable mixture over fish. Bake, uncovered at 325° for 45 minutes or until fish flakes easily when tested with a fork.

Transfer fish to serving platter; spoon vegetables around fish.

Garnish with watercress if desired.

Serve immediately. Yield: 2 servings.

Serve with small red potatoes boiled with butter and parsley, and a mixed salad.

Broiled Fillets of Trout

8 trout fillets
1 tsp. Salt
Dash of pepper
½ C. butter, melted
2 tsp. lemon juice
2 tsp. hot sauce (to your taste)
Fresh parsley sprigs
Lemon slices

Rinse fish thoroughly in cold water. Pat dry. Place skin side up in an aluminum foil lined shallow baking pan. Sprinkle with salt and pepper. Combine butter, lemon juice, and hot sauce. Pour over fish.

Broil 4-5 inchess from heating elements 10 minutes or until fish flakes easily when tested with a fork. Do not turn. Transfer fish to serving platter. Garnish with parsley and lemon.

Yield 4 servings.

Grilled Trout

2 (¾ lb.) dressed trout, butterflied
½ tsp. salt
½ C. butter
2 T. lemon juice
1½ T. hot pepper sauce
Vegetable oil

Rinse fish in cold water. Pat dry. Sprinkle fish with salt.

Place open butterflied fillets on a wire rack. Place another wire rack on top. Secure racks with wires to clamp fish together. (This will prevent fish from breaking apart during grilling.)

Melt butter in a small saucepan. Stir in lemon juice. Remove from heat and stir in hot sauce. Set aside for basting.

Place fish on grill 4-5 inches from medium hot coals. Baste once with oil. Grill 10 minutes or until fish is done, turning often.

Baste frequently with butter mixture. Carefully remove racks, place fish on a warm serving platter and serve.

Yield: 2 servings.

Trout with Almond Lemon Sauce

12 trout fillets (about 2 lbs.)
⅓ C. butter
1 C. lemon juice
½ C. chopped onion
¼ C. hot sauce (pepper)
¼ C. chopped fresh parsley
½ C. sliced almonds
4 eggs, lightly beaten
1 C. milk
2 C. all-purpose flour
1 tsp. pepper
vegetable oil

Rinse fish thoroughly in cold water. Pat dry and set aside.

Combine butter, lemon juice, onion, and hot pepper sauce in a saucepan. Cook over mediumm heat, stirring occasionally until butter melts. Stir in parsley and almonds.

Remove from heat, keep warm.

Combine eggs and mik in a large mixing bowl, beat well. Dip fish in egg mixture, dredge in flour. Sprinkle with pepper.

Fry in ½ inch hot oil (350°) in a large skillet 3 minutes or until golden brown, turning once.

When done, fish should flake easily when tested with fork.

Place fish on warm serving platter. Spoon almond lemon sauce over top. Serve immediately.

Yield: 6 serrvings.

Note: Always drain fish on paper towels after frying.

Pan Fried Seatrout

4 (½ lb.) dressed sea trout
1 tsp. Salt
¼ tsp. Pepper
½ C. all-purpose flour
2 eggs, beaten
1 C. cornmeal
½ C. butter
½ C. vegetable oil
lemon slices
Remoulade Sauce

Rinse fish thoroughly in cold water and pat dry. Sprinkle fish with salt and pepper. Roll fish in flour, dip in egg and dredge in cornmeal.

Heat butter and oil in a large skillet over medium high heat. Add fish and cook until golden brown, turning once. (Fish is done when it flakes easily when tested with a fork.)

Drain well on paper towels. Transfer fish to a serving platter and garnish with lemon slices.

Serve with remoulade sauce (see page 204.)

Yield: 2-4 servings

Albacora Grilhada
Grilled Fresh Tuna

6 half pound tuna steaks, 1 inch thick
½ C. olive oil
juice of one lemon
1 clove carlic minced
fresh ground black pepper

Marinate tuna 1 hour or more. Grill tuna 8-10 minutes or more, basting with additional oil.

Serve with a fish sauce, or melted butter and lemon wedges.

I prefer the tuna to be grilled 6-7 minutes on each side.

Grilled Tuna Steaks

12 (1 inch thick) tuna steaks (about 6 lbs.)
1 C. lemon juice
½ C. soy sauce
2 bay leaves
½ teaspoons dried whole thyme

Rinse steaks thoroughly in cold water, and pat dry. Place steaks in a 15x10x1 inch jelly roll pan.

Combine lemon juice, soy sauce, bay leaves, and thyme, mixing well.

Pour mixture over steaks. Cover and marinate in refrigerator one hour, turning steaks often.

Remove steaks and place in two well greased wire grilling buckets, reserve marinade.

Grill over hot coals 20 minutes or until steaks flake easily when tested with a fork, turning and basting occasionally with reserved marinade.

Serve immediately.

Yield 12 servings.

Oven Baked Tuna

3 lbs. of Tuna
3 T. oil
2 onions
3 garlic cloves
2 tomatoes
1 T. hot pepper paste or hot sauce to taste.
½ tsp cumin
1 T. tomato paste
¼ to ½ C. chopped fresh parsley
1½ C. white wine
salt and pepper to taste.
small potatoes, red or white, cut in half, par boiled about 15 minutes and leave skins on.

Cut the tuna into cubes, about 1½ to 2 inches and roll into oil.

Add the rest of oil, saute the chopped onion and garlic till golden. DO NOT BROWN.

Add chopped tomatos, the tomato paste, pepper past or hot sauce, cumin and parsley. It becomes a thick mixture. Pour the wine and only then season with salt and pepper.

Place potatoes, white or red, around the tuna in a baking pan. Taste to check the seasonings. If necessary, add a little more wine or water to the sauce according to taste.

Place in the oven at 350° for 25 minutes or so. From time to time pour a few spoonsfuls of the gravy over the fish.

Serves 4

Tuna Chowder

3 T. butter
1 medium size onion finely chopped (½ C)
1 stalk celery, finely chopped with leaves
2 medium size carrots, finely diced (1C.)
4 medium size potatoes, diced (4 C.)
2 tsp. salt
¼ tsp. freshly ground black pepper
8 oz. fresh steamed tuna (white)
drained and flaked
4 C. milk.

Melt the butter in a heavy saucepan or dutch oven.

Add the onion, celery, and carrots and cook over low heat, 10 minutes. Add the potatoes and cook 5 minutes.

Add the salt, pepper, and water. Bring to a simmer 20 minutes or until potatoes are tender.

Add tuna and milk and re-heat, but do not boil.

Serve sprinkled with chopped parsley, if you wish.

Hearty enough for a main course if you serve it with a chick pea salad and crusty bread.

Serves 6

Crabmeat With Curried Rice

¾ C. butter
1 C. all-purpose flour
1 qt. milk
1 tsp. salt
¼ tsp. pepper (white)
2 lbs. lump or flake crabmeat
1 C. finely chopped celery
½ C. finely chopped green pepper
½ C. cup chopped pimentos
1 T curry
1½ C. shredded sharp chedder cheese, divided
paprika, curried rice

Melt butter in a medium saucepan. Stir in flour, mixing well. Cook 1 minute, stirring constantly. Gradually add milk, stirring well at medium heat, until thickened and bubbly. Remove sauce from heat. Stir in salt, and pepper. Pour sauce into large mixing bowl. Stir in the crabmeat, celery, green pepper, pimento, and one cup of cheese. Mix well. Pour crabmeat mixture into dish. Top with remaining cheese. Sprinkle with paprika. Bake at 350° for 1 hour. Remove casserole from oven. Serve immediately over curried rice.

Yield: 10-12 servings

Broiled Lobster Tails

4 frozen lobster tails, thawed
½ tsp. salt
¼ tsp. white pepper
2 T. lemon juice, divided
3 T. butter, divided
2 T. bread crumbs
A pinch of paprika and garlic
¾ C. water

Place in a 13x9x2 inch pan. Split lobster tails lengthwise. Cut through upper shell. Peel the meat up leaving attached to end of tail, (the meat is sitting on top of the shell). Brush meat with butter. Sprinkle with garlic, salt, pepper, breadcrumbs, paprika and drizzle juice.

Add water to the bottom of pan, add remaining lemon juice and butter to water.

Broil 4 inches from heating element 4 minutes and additional 3 minutes.

Remove lobster tails to serving platter. Serve with extra melted butter and wedges of lemon.

Yield: 4 servings.

Baked potato and green vegetable is great with this.

Creamed Lobster

½ C. butter
½ C. flour
2 C. whipping cream
2 C. chopped cooked lobster
1 medium size green pepper, chopped
1 whole pimento, chopped
½ tsp. Salt
½ tsp. White pepper

Toast baskets (see page 215.)

Melt butter in a large heavy saucepan over low heat. Add flour, stirring until smooth. Cook 1 minute, stirring constantly.

Gradually add whipping cream. Cook over medium heat, stirring constantly until thickened and bubbly.

Remove from heat. Fold in lobster, green peppers, pimento, salt and pepper.

Spoon ¼ C. mixture into each basket.

Garnish with parsley and serve. Yield: 8 servings.

Shrimp Pie

1 (8oz) can pillsbury crescent rolls
3 eggs slightly beaten
1 T. parmesan cheese
2 C. or 8 oz. Montary Jack cheese cubed.
Enough shrimp, any size, to cover bottom of pie pan.
If you use frozen, be sure that it is throroughly patted dry of any water before placing in pan. One to two bags of frozen may be used.

Cover a 9-10 inch deep pie pan with crescent roll dough.

Cover the bottom with shrimp, shelled and deveined.

Add the cubed cheese and beaten eggs, sprinkle parmesan cheese.

Bake at 350° for 15 minutes. Turn the heat down to 325° for 30-40 minutes.

If crust begins to brown too much, cover edges with aluminum foil.

Let the pie rest for 10 minutes. Serve with a salad of mixed greens.

Shrimp Scampi (#1)

3-4 garlic cloves, minced
¼ C. butter, cubed
¼ C. olive oil
1 lb. uncooked medium shrimp, peeled and deveined.
¼ C. lemon juice
½ tsp. pepper
1 tsp. dried oregano
¼ C. dried bread crumbs
½ C. grated Parmesan cheese
¼ C. minced fresh parsley
Hot cooked angel hair pasta.

Note: Cook pasta to package directions

In a 10 inch oven-proof skillet, saute garlic, butter and oil until tender. Don't let garlic burn. Stir in shrimp, lemon juice, pepper and oregano. Cook and stir for 2-3 minutes or until shrimp turn pink.

Sprinkle with parmesan cheese, bread crumbs and parsley.

Broil 6 inches from heat for 2-3 minutes until topping is golden brown.

Serve over pasta.

Serves 4

Shrimp Scampi (#2)

1 pkg. (10 oz.) Puff pastry shells
1 lb. Large shrimp, shelled and deveined
1 large clove garlic, minced
2 T. butter or olive oil
1 pkg. (1.8 oz) white sauce mix
2 C. milk
½ C. sliced onions
1½ C. quartered cherry tomatoes
½ tsp. dried basil leaves.

Bake pastry shells according to package directions.

In medium saucepan, cook shrimp and garlic in butter until lightly brown.

Cook shrimp in garlic butter - garlic removed. Add sauce mix. Blend in milk, green onions, tomatoes and basil.

Bring to a boil, stirring. Reduce heat and simmer 5 minutes until shrimp is thoroughly cooked.

Spoon mixture into warm pastry shells.

Makes 6 servings

Pratos De Carne De Ovelha
Lamb Dishes

Golden Lamb

2 lbs boneless lamb shoulder, cut into 2-inch cubes
2 C. water
¼ C. chopped fresh celery leaves
2 sprigs fresh parsley
1 bay leaf
2 tsp. salt
3 carrots
3 medium potatoes, peeled and quartered
2 onions, chopped
3 T. watercress
2 T. flour
1 T. medium hot sauce

Combine meat and water, celery, leaves, parsley, bay leaf, and salt in a medium dutch oven. Cover and simmer 1½ hours.

Stir in potatoes and carrots and onion. Cover and simmer an additional 45 minutes or until vegetables are tender.

Combine 3 T. water, flour, and hot sauce. Stir until smooth, stir flour mixture into stew and cook over medium heat util slightly thickened.

Remove the bay leaf and discard.

Serve the stew with a scoop of cooked rice on top.

Broiled Lamb Chops

8 (¾ inch thick) lamb rib chops
1½ tsp. salt
2 T. mustard
½ tsp onion powder
2 T. honey
½ tsp. Pepper

Place chops in a deep container. Sprinkle with salt and water to cover. Let stand 1 hour. Drain well. Place chops on rack in a shallow roasting pan.

Combine all the ingredients, mixing well. Set mixture aside.

Place roasting pan 4-5 inches from heating element. Broil lamb chops 5 minutes on each side.

Brush with mustard sauce mixture. Broil an additional 4 minutes on each side, basting frequently with sauce.

Yield: 4 servings.

Grilled Lamb Chops

4 (1-inch thick) lamb rib chops
2 T. butter softened
1½ tsp. chopped fresh parsley
½ tsp. salt
Dash of pepper
Dash of paprika
1 tsp. lemon juice.

Combine softened butter, parsley, salt, pepper and paprika, mixing until smooth and creamy.

Stir in lemon juice. Spread butter mixture evenly on both sides of chops.

Place chops on grill, grilling 5-6 minutes on each side or until desired degree of doneness.

Yield: 2-4 servings.

Carne De Ovelha Assada
Roast Lamb

1 (3 lbs) lamb shoulder roast
1 lb. New potatoes, peeled and quartered
4-6 carrots, peeled and cut into 3 inch pieces
4 stalks celery, cut into 3 inch pieces
1 (14½ oz) can of tomatoes, undrained
3 C. water
1 T. salt
1 tsp. pepper

Place roast in a greased roasting pan. Arrange potatoes, carrots, and celery in pan.

Combine remaining ingredients, pour over roast. Cover and bake at 350° for 1½ hours.

Uncover and continue baking for 30 minutes or until roast is tender.

Basting frequently with pan drippings, transfer roast and vegetables to a warm serving platter. Let roast rest for 10 minutes before slicing.

Yield: 4 servings.

Braised Lamb Shanks

2 to 2½ lbs lamb shanks
1 T. butter
1 medium onion, chopped
½ C chopped celery
½ C. catsup
½ C. water
2 cloves garlic minced
1½ tsp. Worcestershire sauce
½ tsp. salt
¼ pepper

Heat butter in a large skillet. Add shanks and cook over medium heat until browned. Add onion, celery, catsup, water, garlic, worcestershire sauce, salt, and pepper.

Cover and simmer 1½ hours or until shanks are tender.

Transfer shanks to a warm platter.

Yield: 4 servings

Lamb Stew

2 1/2 lbs. boneless leg of lamb, cubed
8-10 small potatoes, peeled and cut into ½ inch thick slices.
4 medium turnips, peeled and quartered
4 small onions, quartered
4 carrots, scraped and cut into 2 inch pieces
1 (10 oz.) package frozen green peas.
1 can (10 oz.) chick peas
4 C. water
1 tsp. salt
½ tsp pepper

Place all ingredients in a large dutch oven. Cover and cook over low heat for 1½ hours or until meat is tender.

Yield: 4 quarts

Lemon Garlic Leg of Lamb

1 (7-7 ½ lbs) leg of lamb
1½ T. lemon juice
4 cloves garlic, sliced
½ C. all-purpose flour
1 tsp. salt
1 ½ tsp. pepper
1 T. paprika
Mint or currant jelly if you like.

Place lamb fat side up in a shallow roasting pan. Rub surface of lamb with lemon juice.

Make several small slits on outside of lamb and stuff with garlic slices.

Combine flour, salt, pepper adnd paprika. Mix well. Sprinkle flour mixture over lamb, coating well. Insert meat thermometer if desired.

Bake uncovered, at 400° for 15 minutes. Reduce heat to 325°. Continue baking until the desired degree of doneness. A guide for other degrees of doneness is after lowering heat from 400°, continue baking at 140° degrees for one hour and 40° minutes for rare, 160° for 2 hours, medium and 170° for 2 ½ hours for well done.

Transfer lamb to a warm serving platter. Let stand 10 minutes before slicing. Serve lamb with mint or red currant jelly.

Yield: 8 serving.

Roast Lamb and Herbs

1 (7-7 ½ lbs) leg of lamb
3 cloves garlic, minced
1 bay leaf, chushed
1 tsp. salt
½ tsp. pepper
½ tsp. ground ginger
½ tsp. marjoram leaves
½ tsp. rubbed sage
½ tsp. ground thyme
1 T. soy sauce
1 T. vegetable oil.

Place lamb fat side up in a shallow roasting pan. Make several small slits on outside of lamb. Put aside.

Combine remaining ingredients, mix well. Rub mixture over surface of lamb. Insert meat thermometer. Bake uncovered at 450° for 15 minutes. Reduce heat to 350°. Continue baking until desired degree of doneness, using guide for Lemon Garlic lamb if desired.

Transfer to a warm serving platter. Let stand 10 minutes before slicing.

Yield: 8-10 servings.

Roasted Lamb Shoulder

1 (5-6 lb) lamb shoulder roast
1 clove garlic, halved
2 T. olive oil
1 tsp. salt, divided
¾ tsp coarsely ground black pepper, divided
2 C. water
1 T. worchestershire sauce
1 medium onion, chopped
2 T. all-purpose flour

Rub surface of roast with garlic and olive oil. Sprinkle with ¾ tsp salt and ½ tsp. pepper.

Place roast in a large dutch oven, cover and bake at 350° for 1 hour, turning occasionally. Skim fat from pan drippings, discard fat.

Combine water, worchestershire sauce, onion, remaining salt and pepper and pour over roast. Cover and bake 1 hour or until tender.

Transfer roast to a warm serving platter, and keep warm.

Reserve drippings. Combine flour and small amount of water to form a smooth paste. Combine flour mixture and pan drippings in a small saucepan. Cook over medium heat, stirring constantly.

Serve gravy with roast.

Yield 4-6 servings

Serrasco no Espeto
Shish Kabobs

1 (5lb) boneless leg of lamb cut into 1½-inch cubes
1 C. port or other sweet red wine
½ C. vinegar
½ C. olive oil
2 T. lemon juice
2 T. fresh parsley chopped
2 tsp. sugar
1 tsp. dried whole oregano
1 tsp. Salt
½ tsp pepper
1 large onion, chopped
6 cloves garlic, minced
4 medium size green peppers, seeded and cut into 1½-inch pieces
½ lb. fresh mushrooms
1 (10 oz.) package pearl onions
1 pint cherry tomatoes
Hot cooked rice

Combine lamb and the next 11 ingredients in a large shallow container. Cover and marinae in the refrigerator overnight.

Remove lamb from marinade and discard marinade.

Alternate cubes of lamb with green pepper, mushrooms, pearl onions, and tomatoes on skewers.

Place kabobs on grill about 5 inches from medium coals.

Grill 15–20 minutes, turning frequently.

Serve over hot cooked rice.

Yield: 8-10 servings.

Pratos De Porco
Pork Dishes

My husband and I moved to Salisbury in the beginning of the summer. By the end of fall, while having lunch with new friends, the conversation turned to holiday traditions.

Of course, food was the topic.

In my family, roast stuffed pork shoulder with roasted carrots, sweet peas and white potatoes and a green vegetable was the tradition. My friends, in excitement, invited themselves for Christmas dinner as a joke.

A date was set - no need for invitations - for the first week in December.

I broke with tradition and decorated the house. The tree went up and I hoped that it would live until the sixth of January which traditionally is the day of arrival of the Three Kings bearing gifts, ending the holidays.

With the decoration done, menu in hand, I went shopping.

At the meat counter, I looked for a fesh pork shoulder. It was not to be found. I rang the bell, and from the back came the butcher, greeting me with "Hello, how can I help you?"

"Hello, I am looking for a fresh pork shoulder. Also, can you remove the bone, leaving a pocket?"

"Yes, it can be done, but I don't have it."

I thanked him and left.

By the time I arrived at the fourth store, I pressed the button again, and the butcher came to the counter. So I began by saying, "I hope you can help me. I see you have beautiful cuts of pork, but what I need is a fresh pork shoulder about 15 pounds," while at the same time pointing to my shoulder. "Can you remove the bone leaving a pocket?"

He paused, then, as if a light bulb went on in his head, said, "Oh. Yes I can, but what you want is a leg of fresh ham."

"Thank you so much, but is not ham the process you do to pork meat?"

He smiled and said, "Yep! In Salisbury, you gotta ask for fresh ham if you want to get it."

"I will do that. Thank you."

Thinking leg of pork it is, home I went with a very nice, de-boned leg of pork.

Broiled Pork Chops

4 (1½ inch thick) pork loin chops
½ tsp. salt
¼ tsp. pepper and garlic powder
Hot cooked noodles of your choice

Sprinkle chops with salt and pepper, and garlic powder. Place on a rack in broiler pan, 3-4 inches from heat. Broil 5-6 minutes on first side. Turn and broil 3 minutes or until browned. Transfer chops to a warm serving platter of hot cooked noodles.

Reserve pan drippings for saucepan.

Sauce
Pan drippings
3 T. chopped yellow onion
2 T. butter
3 T. fresh lemon juice
¾ tsp tarragon
2 T. all-purpose flour
1 C. milk
2 T. Dijon mustard
1 tsp. salt
½ tsp. pepper

Saute onion in butter in a medium saucepan until tender. Add all ingredients, bring to a boil, 10 minutes, stirring frequently.

Pour sauce over chops and noodles and serve.

Yield: 1 Cup

Cranberry Glazed Pork Chops

1 C. water
1 C. sugar
2 C. fresh cranberries
6 (1-inch thick) pork chops
½ C. all-purpose flour
2 T. butter
6 medium size sweet potatoes, (optional)

Combine water and sugar in a medium saucepan. Bring to a boil. Reduce heat, simmer 10 minutes. Add cranberries. Bring to a boil. Remove from heat and set aside.

Dredge pork chops in flour

Brown in butter in a large skillet. Drain chops and place in a 13x9x2 inch baking dish. Pour glaze over chops.

Cover and bake at 350° for 30 minutes. Uncover and bake 30 minutes or until chops are tender.

Cook potatoes in oven with chops at 350° for one hour.

If desired, mash the potatoes with butter and place a large cup of sweet potatoes on the plate with chop on top. Spoon glaze over chops. Serve with a green salad.

Serves 6.

Pork Chops Supreme

4 (1-inch) thick pork chops
1 onion, sliced in circles
1 lemon, sliced in circles
catsup
salt and pepper

Heat oven to 350°. Put 4, 1-inch thick pork chops in a baking dish, salt and pepper well.

Top chops with a slice of onion, then a round slice of lemon.

Sprinkle generously with brown sugar. Pour 1 tsp. catsup over each chop.

Cover and bake for 1 hour. Uncover and bake 30 minutes longer.

Porco Rechiado
Pork Stuffed Eggplant

2 medium eggplants
1 medium size green pepper, chopped fine
1 medium onion, chopped
2 T. butter
2 medium tomatoes, seedless , peeled and chopped
1 C. diced, baked pork, (left over)
⅛ tsp pepper and salt to taste
½ C. chopped green olives
¼ C. soft breadcrumbs.

Wash eggplant. Cut into 2 lengthwise halves. Remove pulp, leaving a firm shell. Chop pulp and set aside.

Cook eggplant shells in boiling salted water to cover 5 minutes or until tender but firm.

Drain, cool slightly.

Saute green pepper, onion and reserved eggplant pulp in butter in a large skillet until tender.

Stir in tomato, pork meat, soft and pepper. Cook 1 minute or until thoroughly heated.

Place shells in a 12x8x2 inch baking pan. Spoon eggplant mixture into shells. Top with bread crumbs.

Bake at 350° for 20 minutes or until lightly bown.

Yield: 4 servings.

Marinated Pork Roast

½ C. soy saucepan
½ C. dry sherry
1 T. dry mustard
1 tsp. ground ginger
1 tsp. dried whole thyme
2 cloves garlic, minced
1 (3-4 lbs.) pork loin roast, boned, rolled and tied.
large bay leaf (optional)

Combine the first 7 ingredients. Stir well. Place in a zip lock bag with the meat and marinate roast overnight in refrigerator, turn occasionally.

Remove roast to a well-greased rack in a shallow roasting pan, reserving marinade. Insert meat thermometer at an angle into thickest part of roast.

Bake uncovered at 325° for 2 hours and 45 mintes or until meat thermometer registers 170°. Baste with reserved mariande every 15 minutes durung last 45 minutes of cooking time.

Remove roast to serving platter. Let roast stand 10-15 minutes before slicing.

Serves 12

Pork Roast

1 tsp. salt, divided
¾ tsp pepper divided
garlic powder
1 (2 ½ -3 lb.) pork loin end roast
¼ C. all purpose flour
¼ C. melted butter
3 T. vegetable oil
1 large onion cut into four pieces
6 carrots, peeled cut into 2 inch pieces
6 medium potatoes, peeled and halved.
vegetable or olive oil for cooking

Rub half of the salt pepper and garlic over surface of the roast. Dredge roast in flour. Brown roast on all sides in butter and oil in a large deep cast iron skillet. (Iron is best.)

Remove roast from skillet and drain on paper towels.

Place roast over onions. Add carrots and potatoes. Sprinkle remaining salt, pepper and garlic over vegetables.

Cover and bake at 350° for 1½ hours or until meat thermometer registers 170°. Transfer roast to a serving platter. Rest 15 minutes.

Drain vegetables and place around roast. Slice and serve.

Note: a roasting pan will do. Cover with aluminum foil. Uncover for the last 30 minutes.

Pork Loin Roast

1 (4 to 5 lb.) pork loin roasting
1 tsp. salt
½ tsp pepper
2 T all-purpose flour
2 medium onions, chopped
1 carrot, cut into ½ inch slices
1 stalk celery
7-8 large sprigs fresh parsley
½ tsp. dried thyme leaves
1 bay leaf, crushed
4 C. water, divided
⅓ C. firmly packed brown sugar
2 T. all purpose flour
1-1½ C. water, divided

Rub roast with salt and pepper. Dust with 3 T. flour. Place roast, fat side up on rack in a roasting pan. Insert meat thermometer, making certain thermometer does not touch bone or fat.

Place onions, carrot, celery and parsley around meat. Sprinkle meat with thyme and bay leaf. Pour 2 C. water on roasting pan. Add remaining 3 C. water as need for basting.

Roast pork at 350° for 2½ hours or until roast reaches 170°, basting often with juices in pan. Sprinkle brown sugar over roast during last 30 minutes of baking. Let stand 10 to 15 minutes.

Remove roast, parsley, carrot and celery. Reserve pan drippings. Combine 2 T. flour and 1-1½ C. water. Stir until smooth. Pour flour mixture into pan drippings. Cook, stirring constantly until thickened and bubbly.

Serve gravy with roast. Serve with glazed fried apples.

Yield 6-8 servings.

Bifes De Porco Con Ananas
Pineapple Pork Chops

1 (8 oz.) can pineapple chunks undrained
5 slices white bread, cubed
¼ C. chopped onion
¼ C. chopped celery
3 T. butter melted
1 tsp. salt, divided
¼ tsp. rubbed sage
⅛ tsp. ground cinnamon
6 (¾-inch thick) pork chops

Drain pineapple, reserving 3 T. juice.

Combine pineapple chunks, bread cubes, onion, celery, butter, ½ tsp. Salt, sage, and cinnamon in a large bowl, mixing well. Set stuffing mixture aside.

Place pork chops in a 13x9x2 inch baking dish and sprinkle with reserve pineapple juice and remaining salt.

Top pork chops evenly with stuffing mixture.

Cover and bake at 350° for 30 minutes.

Uncover and bake an additional 15-20 minutes or until chops are tender.

Yield: 6 servings.

Carne De Porco Assada
Roast Pork with Dressing

3 green apples peeled and chopped fine
4 C. breadcrumbs
¼ C. plus 2 T. butter melted
1 T. oil
1 C. chopped onion
¾ tsp. Salt
¼ tsp. Pepper
½ tsp. Dried thyme
¼ tsp. Sage.
1 (6 lb.) pork shoulder roast, deboned and cut with pocket
¾ C. water

In a skillet, add oil, chopped onion and aples. Saute until the onion is soft, not brown.

Combine breadcumbs, butter, onion, apples, salt, pepper, thyme and sage. Mix well. Stuff pocket of roast with breadcrumb mixture, then tie with string to secure opening if desired.

Place roast and water in a lightly greased shallow roasting pan. Insert meat thermometer in the thickest part of roast. Bake at 350° for 2-3 hours, or until thermometer registers 170. Baste occasionally with pan drippings. Let roast rest 10-15 minutes before slicing.

Transfer roast to a serving platter.

Varias Receitas
Other Recipes

Guisado De Favas con Chouriço
Sauteed Favas with Sausages

8 C. fresh favas
2 onions chopped
3 cloves of garlic, chopped
4 T. olive oil
1 T. vinegar
3-4 T. tomato sauce
3 carrots, chopped into small pieces
6 hot Italian sausages

Saute the onions and carrots in olive oil. When the onion is translucent, add the garlic, sautee 2 minutes. Add vinegar, tomato sauce, sausage, and favas. Add enough water to cover. Bring to boil, then turn the heat down and simmer for 25 minutes, or until favas are tender.

Add parsley and let stand for 10-15 minutes.

Serve with rustic bread and a glass of red wine.

Note: In the original recipe, the chouriço is cut in ½ inch slices and sauteed. The Italian sausages fall apart so I cook them first whole, then cut the sausage into ½ inch slices and add to favas.

Macaroni and Cheese with Truffle Oil

4 T. unsalted butter
4 T. all purpose flour
3½ C. warm milk
½ tsp. Kosher salt and pepper to taste
3 C. extra sharp chedder cheese, shredded
4 oz. Goat cheese, cut up
2 T. truffle oil, (optional)
8 oz. Macaroni uncooked
½ C. grated Parmesan cheese

Preheat the broiler to 400°.

Spray a 4 qt. casserole dish or pie plate with cooking spray.

In a small saucepan, melt butter. Stir in flour and mix together to form a roux. Add half of the warm milk. Using a whisk to make sure you get the sides and bottom of saucepan. Mix well as you add rest of milk.

Stirring the side of pot, cook 5-6 minutes. Do not boil. Add salt, pepper, chedder cheese and goat cheese into the sauce. Mix until completely melted and smooth.

Add the truffle oil (optional) and mix well. Cover and set aside.

Cook macaroni according to package directions. Place the cooked and drained macaroni in a large bowl and pour the cheese mixture over it, mixing well. Spoon into a casserole dish or a deep dish pie plate. Sprinkle Parmesan cheese over top and broil until the top is crusty and golden, approximately 6-10 minutes depending on your broiler. Watch it carefully and be careful not to burn it, and serve.

Note: The same recipe leaving the truffle oil out, add a cup to a pound of crab meat before broiling. It's delicious!

Ervilhas Guisadas a Portuguesa
Peas Portuguese Style

2 T. butter
½ C. finely chopped onions
¼ C. chicken stock, fresh or canned
3 C. cooked fresh peas, about 3 lbs. (You can substitute 3 ten oz. Package frozen peas. Thoroughly defrost but not cooked.)
¼ C. finely chopped parsley
¼ C. finely chopped fresh coriander leaves (cilantro)
½ tsp. sugar
salt to taste
freshly ground black pepper
4 oz. Linquiça, or chorizo (or substitute other garlic seasoned smoked pork sausage. Cut into ¼ inch slices.)
4 eggs

In a heavy 10 inch skillet or shallow casserole, melt the butter over moderate heat.

When the foam has almost subsided, add the onions and stirring frequently, cook for 8-10 minutes, or until they are lightly colored.

Stir in stock, freshly cooked or frozen peas, parsley, coriander, sugar, ¼ tsp. Salt and a few grindings of pepper and overlap the sausage slices around the edge of the skillet. Bring to a boil over high heat the reduce heat to low, cover and simmer for 5 minutes.

Break 1 egg into a saucer, and holding the dish close to the pan, slide the egg on top of the peas. One at a time, slide the other eggs into the pan, keeping them well apart. Sprinkle them lightly with salt and pepper. Cover the skillet and cook for 3-4 minutes until the egg yolks are covered with an opaque film and the whites are set.

Serve at once, directly from the skillet.

Chouriço Con Ervilhas
Sausage and Peas

1 onion chopped
¼ C. vegetable oil
1 tsp. paprika
1 tsp. salt
pepper to taste
3 C. peas, fresh or frozen
water enough to cover chouriço or other hot sausage, 1 package

Cook peas.

Saute onions in oil. Add the chauriço. Cook whole. Add paprika, cook on low heat.

Serve with a good hearty crusted bread in a bowl with chopped parsley.

Mexican Chorizo can be substituted for chourico. Cook whole sausage if using chorizo and then cut into pieces

Carne Con Feijão E Vinho
Portuguese Chili

3 lbs. beef, pork and lamb (1 lb. each)
2 large onions chopped
3 cloves garrlic chopped
4 T. olive oil
1 C. water
1½ C. wine, red or white.
2 T. beef base
2 T. chilli powder or red pepper flakes is a good substitute for calda da pimenta
4 tsp. oregano
1 T. ground cumin
salt to taste
4 cans (1 lb.) red kidney beans
2 large cans chopped tomatoes.

The meat is cut into cubes, not ground.

Saute beef,pork and lamb, onion, garlic in oil until browned. Add water, wine, beef base and seasonings.

Simmer one or two hours, add beans with liquid. Simmer 15 minutes to heat beans. If chili is to watery, add 1 can beans mashed.

Taste and adjust for flavor.

Note: I use Members Mark Tones Beef Base. Make the day before serving. It's best the second day.

Chouriço Con Feijão & Arroz
Chouriço with Rice and Beans

1 (16oz.) package dried red kidney beans
10 C. water
½ C. vegetable oil
1 medium onion, chopped
1 medium size green pepper, chopped
2 stalks celery, chopped
2 tsp. salt
2 tsp. sugar
1 tsp. garlic powder.
¾ tsp red pepper
½ tsp. dried parsley flakes
2 C. chouriço, may substitute with Italion sausages or chorizo cooked, skin removed, cut into 1 ends.
hot cooked rice.

Wash beans. Combine beans and next 10 ingredients in a dutch oven.

Bring to a boil. Reduce heat, cook uncovered over medium heat, 1½ hours or until beans are tender.

Stir in sausage. Cook 30 minutes.

Serve over hot cooked rice. Yield 6-8 servings.

Note: To speed the process, the day before add the beans to 12 C. of water, bring to a boil. turn the heat off and let it stand over night. The next day, drain water and proceed.

Panquecas

Pancakes for A Special Sunday Breakfast

My mother was given the recipe for pancakes approximately in the mid 1960s.

The first time pancakes were served to my grandmother, she asked what is this bread? My mother explained, "It's little, small, raised flat bread."

She liked the softness of the bread served with the sweets. From that day on, no matter how many times we served her pancakes, she always called them, "sweet flat bread."

Panquecas
Plain Pancakes

¼ C. butter
½ C. sifted powdered sugar
1 egg
1½ C. all-purpose flour
2 tsp. baking powder
¼ tsp. baking soda
⅔ C. milk
vegetable oil for griddle
1 tsp sugar

Cream butter in a medium mixing owl. Gradually add sugar, beating well. Add egg. Mix well.

Combine flour, baking powder, and soda. Stir well. Add to creamed mixture, alternately with milk, beginning and ending with flour mixture.

Drop batter by heaping tablespoonfuls, onto a medium hotlightly greased griddle or skillet. Cook until tops of pancakes are covered with bubbles and edges appear slightly dry. Turn and continue cooking until bottom sides are browned.

Serve hot or cold. Yield: about 3½ dozen.

Great with honey, butter, fruits and preserves

Panquecas (#2)
Cornmeal Pancakes

½ C. cornmeal
1½ C. boiling water
1 C. milk
2¼ C. all purpose flour
1 T. baking powder
⅓ C. powdered sugar
1½ sp. Salt
2 eggs beaten
3 T. butter melted
vegetable oil for griddle

Combine cornmeal and water in a large mixing bowl. Stir well. Set aside for 5 minutes.

Gradually add milk to cornmeal mixture, stirring well. Sift together flour, baking powder, sugar, and salt. Stir into cornmeal mixture.

Add beaten eggs and melted butter. Stir well.

Drop batter by 2 tablespoonfuls onto a medium hot, lightly greased griddle.

(Stir mixture frequently to prevent cornmeal from settling.)

Turn pancakes when tops are browned. Serve hot with your favorite topping.

Yield: About 2 dozen.

Pancakes

3 T. unsalted butter, more for serving
2½ C. unbleached all purpose flour
¼ C. granulated sugar
1½ tsp. baking powder
½ tsp. baking soda
½ tsp. kosher salt
2 C. buttermilk
2 large eggs
vegetable oil for griddle
pure maple sugar syrup for servings

Melt the butter. Set aside to cool slightly. In a large bowl, whisk the flour, sugar, baking powder, baking soda and salt.

In a medium bowl, whisk the buttermilk and eggs. Pour the wet ingredients into the dry ingredients. Whisk the buttermilk and eggs.

Pour the wet ingredients into the dry ingredients. Whisk gently until the dry ingredients are almost incorporated. Stop before the batter is evenly moistened.

Add the cooled melted butter and mix just until the batter is evenly moistened. There will be lumps. Let the batter rest while you heat the griddle.

Heat the skillet on medium heat. Lightly oil the griddle. Pour ¼ C. for each pancake.

Panquecas De Bananas
Spiced Banana Pancakes

ground allspice
¾ tsp. Freshly round black pepper
1¼ C. butter
2 T. packed brown sugar
1 egg
1½ C. all purpose flour
2 tsp. baking powder
¼ tsp. Baking soda
⅔ C. milk
4 medium bananas sliced in 1-inch pieces

Cream butter in a medium mixing bowl. Gradually add sugar beating well. Add egg and beat well.

Combine flour, baking powder soda, spices and stir well.

Add to creamed mixture alternately with milk, beginning and ending with flour mixture.

Drop batter by heaping tablespoonfuls onto a medium hot, lightly greased griddle or skillet. Cook until tops of pancakes are covered with bubbles and edges appear slightly dry. Turn and continue cooking until bottom and sides are browned.

Serve hot with sliced bananas on top.

Yield: About 3½ dozen.

Panquecas De Familia
Family Pancake Recipe

1 egg
½ tsp. salt
2 T. oil
1 C. flour
½ C cornmeal
3 tsp. baking powder
1½ T. sugar
1½ C. milk
1½ tsp. vanilla
butter for the pan

In a large bowl, beat together all wet ingredients.

In a second bowl, mix dry ingredients.

Add dry to the wet ingredients and stir just until combined.

Heat a 10-inch skillet to medium heat. Melt butter. Pour ¼ C. of batter per pancake on griddle.

Flip once it starts to bubble and turn golden brown.

Repeat until you have a stack of pancakes.

Serve right away with butter or with real maple syrup

May add blueberries or strawberries. If using berries, do not mix in batter. Place on top of batter once it is on griddle.

Panquecas De Mistura
Mix Pancakes

1 tsp. baking soda
2 C. buttermilk
1½ C cornmeal
½ C. all-purpose flour
2 T. sugar
2 eggs beaten
2 T. vegetable oil (or butter melted)
maple syrup goes well with these

Dissolve soda in buttermilk. Stir well.

Combine dry ingredients. Add eggs and buttermilk mixing well. Add oil, mixing well.

Pour ¼ C. batter onto a medium hot, lightly greased griddle.

Turn pancakes when tops are covered with bubbles and edges or browned.

Serve hot with butter and syrup if desired.

Yield: 1 ½ dozen.

Overnight Sensation For Christmas Morning

(Not pancakes, but great for special occasions)

6 slices Italian bread, buttered on both sides
1 lb. Longhorn cheese, grated (may substitute favorite cheese)
2 C. half and half
1 lb. sausage cooked and drained (May use your favorite sausage)
6 eggs

Butter a 9x13 inch baking dish. Put in bread.

Spread sausage over bread, add cheese, and spread evenly.

Beat eggs and half and half, pour over sausage and cheese layers.

Refrigerate over night.

Bake uncovered 40 minutes at 350°. Serve hot.

Serves 6-8

Saladas
Salads

There is dining ... then there is savoring food from the kitchen table. Your life is just as unique. The way you care for those you love and how you choose to eat.

Most of the time salad is consumed after the main dish.

Salada
Salad

Basic bib lettuce.
White or red onion sliced
Hard boiled eggs, ½ per person
olives, your favorite
Arrange in individual dishes

Arrange 3 bib lettuce leaves and ½ hard boiled egg in center of plate with sliced onions, olives, oil, vinegar or lemon juice.

Each persons drizzles their salad with oil and vinegar, salt and pepper on the table.

All through Europe bib lettuce is the most popular for salads.

Salada (#2)

1 red bell pepper
1 green bell pepper
3 plum tomatoes
¼ C. olive oil
1 cucumber, peeled
¼ C. flat leaf parsley
2 T. chili paste if you don't have calda de pimenta
salt and pepper to taste

Turn the broiler on and set the peppers underneath. Cook turning occasionally until lightly blackened on all sides.

Repeat with the tomatoes, but first lightly coat the tomatoes in olive oil. They cook faster.

Remove when lightly blackened all over and add the peppers and tomatoes in a ziplock bag. This will steam the skins off. Rub off skin with a dish towel or paper.

Let cool on tray.

Peel and slice the cucumbers. Chop the peppers (seeds removed) into 1-inch squares.

Toss the chopped bell peppers, tomato and cucumbers in a large bowl.

Add chopped parsley, olive oil, red wine vinegar and chili pepper.

Season with salt and pepper. Set in the fridge overnight for the flavors to really marry.

Remove from fridge 3 minutes before serving.

Salada De Repolho
Cabbage Salad

1 cabbage
4-5 carrots
3-4 cucumbers, seeds removed
¾ C. sugar
¾ C. vinegar
½ C. oil
3 tsp. Each salt and pepper
½ C. green or red pepper
1 large onion, sweet

Cut cabbage into their slices, grated carrots and chopped onion

Cut cucumber into 4 long lengths and remove seeds.

Cut into chunks and slice chopped peppers cut into thick slices.

Add vinegar, oil, salt and pepper. Toss and keep in the fridge for at least 24 hours. Toss 3 or 4 times during the 24 hours.

Chick Peas Vinagrette

2 cans (20 oz) chick peas, drained and rinsed
1 large red onion, thinly skinned or cut into rings
1 cup (4 oz.) tiny cubes gruyier cheese
⅔ C. olive or vegetable oil
¼ C. red wine vinegar
1 clove garlic, crushed
¼ tsp. Salt
⅛ tsp. ground black pepper
¼ C. finely chopped fresh chives or 4 tsp freeze dried.
¼ C. chopped fresh parsley
2 hard cooked eggs
2 T. drained capers optional

Place the chick peas, onion and cheese in a medium size bowl.

In a screw cap jar, combine the oil, vinegar, garlic, salt, pepper, chives, parsley, chopped, white of the egg and capers. Shake to mix.

Pour enough of the dressing over the salad to coat when tossed.

Cover and chill several hours. Serve in lettuce lined bowl with finely sieved egg yolk as garnish.

Grão De Bico Com Couve
Chickpea and Kale Salad

1 (28 oz.) can chickpeas, rinsed and drained
5 T. extra virgin olive oil
½ tsp. Ground cumin
½ tsp. Paprika
kosher salt and freshly ground black pepper
1 small bunch curly kale, trimmed and thinly sliced, about 1 qt. of greens
½ C. pine nuts
½ C. sun dried tomatoes, thinly sliced
1 medium clove of garlic, grated (about 1 tsp.)
4 scallions, white and light green parts only, thinly sliced.
2 T. juice and 1 tsp. zest from 1 lemon, plus more juice as desired
½ tsp. hot sauce (as you like)
2 tsp. sherry or red wine vinegar
1 C. fresh parsley, roughly chopped
1 C. fresh mint leaves, roughly chopped.

Adjust oven racks upper and lower, middle positions and pre heat oven to 350°.

Line a rimmed baking sheet with paper towels.

Spread chickpeas on top and roll around under your hands to thoroughly dry.

Transfer chickpeas to a large bowl. Add 1 T. olive oil, cumin and paprika. Season to taste with salt and pepper.

Discard paper towels and line baking sheet with aluminum foil.

Spread chickpeas over foil and transfer to oven. Roast on upper rack, shaking pan occasionally until chickpeas are about ¾ their original size with dense, nutty texture, about 1 hour.

Remove from oven and let cool slightly.

Meanwhile, add kale to now empty chickpea bowl. Add 1 T. olive oil. Season with salt and pepper and massage kale until well coated in oil. Set aside.

Place pine nuts in a skillet and transfer to lower rack of oven. Toast, stirring occasionally until pine nuts are deep golden brown, about 15 minutes.

Remove from oven and transfer to a bowl. Set aside.

In a medium bowl, combine sun dried tomatoes, scallions, garlic, lemon juice, zest, hot sauce, vinegar and remaining 3 T. oil. Season with salt and pepper and stir with a fork.

When chickpeas are cooked and slightly cooled, add to bowl with kale.

Add pine nuts, sun dried tomatoes, parsley and mint.

Toss with hands until well combined.

Adjust seasoning with more salt and pepper or lemon if necessary.

Chick Pea and Rice Salad

Dressing:
¾ C. olive oil or vegetable oil
¼ C. red wine vinegar
2 T. lemon juice
½ tsp. salt
¼ tsp. freshly ground black pepper
1 clove garlic, crushed
⅓ tsp. crushed hot red pepper flakes

Salad:
4 C. cooked rice, (1¼ C. raw)
1 can (1 lb. 14 oz.) chick peas, rinsed and drained
1 large green pepper, seeded and chopped
2 stalks celery, chopped
1 pint cherry tomatoes, halved
1 can (15 oz) pitted black olives, sliced
3 T. chopped fresh parsley
2 hard boiled eggs, sliced (optional)

In a screw cap jar or small bowl, combine oil, vinegar, lemon juice, salt, pepper, garlic and red pepper flakes. Shake or beat to blend.

In a salad serving bowl, combine the rice, chick peas, green pepper, celery, tomatoes, olives, and parsley. Toss.

Add dressing to moisten, and chill several hours. Garnish with egg slices if you wish.

Salada De Cove
Kale Salad

Dressing:
5 T. extra virgin olive oil
Kosher salt and freshly ground black pepper
⅔ C. mayonnaise
6 anchovy fliets
1 medium clove garlic, minced, about 1 tsp.
1½ oz. Parmigiano cheese, finely grated (¾ C.)
2 T. lemon juice
1 small white onion or shallots finely sliced
5 oz. hearty bread, roughly torn into 1 inch pieces.
Your favorite kale (stems removed)

In a large bowl, massage kale with 3 T. olive oil making sure to coat all surfaces, kneading with our hands to help break down the tougher pieces about 2 minutes. Set aside.

Prepare the croutons and the dressing.

Combine bread pieces with remaining olive oil in bowl of a food processor.

Pulse until broken down into pea size pieces. Season to taste with salt and pepper and pulse once or twice to combine.

Transfer to a rimmed baking sheet. Place in oven and bake until croutons are golden brown.

Add all ingredients. Let salad rest for about 30 minutes and serve.

Condiments, Relishes, Glazes, Marinades, and Sauces

Are you looking for a special sauce, glaze, or marinade for meat or seafood? Maybe a homemade condiment or relish?

Super Simple Vinaigrette

A 3-1 ratio oil to vinegar makes for a perfectly smooth, thick immersion. Add shallots finely chopped. Add a teaspoon of mustard, salt and pepper. Stir and serve.

Molho De Tomate
My Grandmother's Ketchup

1 box of ripened tomatoes
6 C. vinegar
8 onions
2 C. sugar
6 red peppers (sweet)
½ C. salt

Chop or grind onions and peppers. Add to tomatoes, stew and press through colander, then add rest of the ingredients. Bring to a boil, turn heat to low and cook until it is thick.

Seal while hot into glass jars.

This is a direct translation.

I remember my mother and sometimes some of my aunts gathering at my grandmother's house and making ketchup. The long kitchen table was covered with ketchup jars, enough for the year.

My father came with baskets to carry it home.

I don't plan to make ketchup any time soon! We have great products in the market.

Homemade Mayonnaise

3 egg yolks
1 tsp. Salt
2 C. vegetable oil
2 T. white vinegar

Beat yolks and salt in a deep narrow bowl at high speed with an electric mixer until thick and light lemon colored.

Add oil in a thin, steady stream. Beat until mixture begins to thicken.

Gradually add vinegar, beating until thicken.

Spoon mayonnaise into a glass or plastic container. Cover container and refrigerate.

Yield: About 2 cups.

Mustard Sauce

⅓ C. commercial sour cream
⅓ C. mayonaise
1 T. dry mustard
2 green onions, chopped very fine.

Combine all ingredients in a small bowl. Stir well. Cover and refrigerate until thoroughly chilled. Great for dipping.

Yield: ¾ C.

Hot Sweet Mustard

¼ C. dry mustard
⅔ C. water divided
¼ C. sugar

1½ T. cornstarch
½ tsp. salt
⅓ C. vinegar

Add all together and stir. Also can do a small serving.

2 T. dry mustard
1 tsp. oil
1 tsp sugar

Enough water to make the thickness you like. Add all ingredients and stir.

A good tip is to have dry mustard powder in the pantry. Mustard powder is also known as Ingles mustard. It keeps a couple of years.

Comes in handy when you run out of mustard in the middle of cooking. No need to run to the store.

Molho De Mostarda
Mustard Sauce

2 whole eggs and 1 egg yolk
1 T. dry mustard
2 T. vinegar
¼ C. olive oil
¼ tsp. salt, pepper, paprika to taste
light cream to thin

Beat eggs and egg yolk well. Beat in seasoning and greadually add vinegar and oil, beating constantly.

Cook over boiling water or in double boiler over water until thick, stirring constantly.

Add cream to thin if desired.

Calda De Pimentos or Pasta De Pimentos Pepper Paste

Wear gloves to be safe. Wash peppers. Remove stems and seeds.

In a large pot, cover pepper with water, bring to a boil.

Reserve 2 or 3 cups of water. Set aside.

Drain water and let peppers cool.

In a blender, set on medium. Blend peppers. Use a bit of water if needed.

Add salt to taste, return paste to a low heat. Stir constantly. Bring to a boil. Remove from heat.

Set aside for fermentation about 2-3 days.

Fill clean jars, leaving about 1-inch. Tightly close lids.

Use as pepper sauce.

Keep on shelf and refrigerate after opening.

Olives

A lesser known product is the much loved olive.

In the Azores, there are some olive trees, mostly in Terceira and Pico Islands.

The harvest is done by hand, placed in a bag that is tied to the waist, estimating one bag holds about 4-5 Kg.

When full, the olives are then deposited in wicker bastkets with a handle on each side. The basket holds about 40 Kg. Of olives.

It takes a man one day to pick a basket of olives.

The olives then are thrown into a tub called a mash tub, full of water for 10 days. The water is changed daily.

The mash tub holds 200 liters of water, 150 kg of olives and 15 kg. of salt.

After the 10th day, the olives are placed in layers, alternating with garlic, bay leaf, and oregano. The tub is covered with a sack cloth bag, tied around the mash tub for the curing brine.

After 3 months, it is ready to be served.

We enjoy olives without thinking of the work and time it takes to produce them.

On most Azorian kitchen tables, a jar of olives and jar of pickles are always there. Olives are used in many dishes.

Pimenta Moida
Pepper Relish

Wash peppers well. Let them drain. (Use rubber gloves for this process.)

Remove stems by pushing the stem in and pulling out. The stem and seeds comes out easily.

Cut pepper into 4 quarters. Grind by hand, using a hand grinder or a food processer.

Use a generous amount of salt. Set aside to ferment 24-48 hours or until it stops fermenting.

Stir 2 or 3 times a day.

Fill jars leaving about ¾ to 1 inch at the top. Invert the jar to keep on the shelf, or cover the top with vegetable oil and close the lid tight.

Note: Pepper Relish or Pepper Paste used with garlic and onion. You have the trinity of Azorian cooking.

Cortume De Pimenta
Pickled Peppers

Remove stems and seeds.

Use the same process as in pepper relish.

Boil water, 1 C. to 1 C. vinegar and ⅓ C. salt. Make as much as needed.

Fill jars with peppers. Cover with the brine. Leave about 1 inch from the top.

Note: For this, I like the long thin peppers like mild banana peppers.

Pimenta Salgada
Salted Peppers

Use the same process of cleaning peppers as in Pepper Relish.

Pack the peppers in layers with salt in between until jar is full. It will pack down some.

Then cover the peppers with 1 C. of salt to 2 cups of water.

Note: To use the salted peppers, wash well and let stand in fresh water to remove most of the salt. Use kosher salt, not fine salt.

Relish De Pero Applesauce Relish (short cut)

1 can (13 oz) applesauce
1-2 T. horseradish
Dash of nutmeg

Combine well and serve cold with hot meat, especially pork.

Cranberry Orange Chutney

1 C. fresh orange sections
1 C. cranberries
1 C. chopped unpeeled apples
½ tsp. Ground ginger
½ tsp. Cinnamon
¼ C. chopped walnuts
½ C. orange juice
2 C. sugar
¼ C. raisons
1 tsp. Vinegar

Combine all ingredients in a large saucepan and bring to a boil. Reduce heat and simmer 5 or 10 minutes or until berries begin to burst. Pour into sterilized jars and store in the refrigerator. Will keep for several months.

Good to serve with roast pork.

Glaze

¼ C. honey
1 T. orange juice
2 T. chopped fresh mint leaves

Combine all ingredients; stir well. Great with lamb or ham.

Yield: about ¼ C.

Cranberry Glaze

2 medium oranges
1 C. whole berry cranberry sauce
1 C. orange juice
½ tsp. ground ginger
2 T. grated orange rind

Peel oranges. Discard seeds and white membranes. Chop pulp; set aside.

Combine cranberry sauce, ginger, and orange rind in medim saucepan. Add orange pulp, mixing well.

Cook over low heat until thoroughly heated, stirring occasionally.

Yield: About 2 cups.

Good with pork or chicken.

Apricot Glaze

¼ C. sugar
¼ lb. Dried apricots
1 C. water

Add sugar, apricots and water. Cook gently until tender and thick.

Strain through fine sieve. If too thick, dilute with water. Bottle while hot until ready to use.

Use to glaze coffee cakes or to glaze open fruit pies or tarts.

Custard Glaze

2 eggs, well beaten
½ C. sugar
1 tsp. vanilla
2 T. milk or cream

Stir eggs well and add all ingredients in top of a double boiler over gently boiling water on medium heat. Stir constantly until all ingredients are cooked and thick and creamy. Mix well and use to glaze tarts or fruit pies.

Can be poured on bread or cake hot or cold.

Glaze for Lamb

½ C. orange marmalade
3 T. lemon juice
1 T. brown sugar
2 tsp. prepared mustard

Combine all ingredients in a small heavy saucepan over medium heat.

Bring to a boil, stirring constantly. Remove from heat.

Yield: ½ C.

Honey Glaze

¼ C. honey
1 T. orange juice
2 T. chopped fresh mint leaves

Combine all ingredients; stir well.

Yield: about ¼ C.

Glaze for Tenderloin Pork

Melt 8 oz. currant or apple jelly with 1 T. soy sauce and 2 T. sherry. Cook for a couple of minutes stirring. When tenderloin is done, remove from oven and spoon glaze over.

I find ½ of recipe is enough for basting, but you may drizzle over slices before serving.

Vinha D'Alhos Marinade

½ C. water
½ C. red wine
A little pepper sauce or hot as you like, garlic, onion, chopped parsley
1 tsp. tomato paste
1 T. vegetable oil

Mix all together. Keep in a glass jar in the fridge. Use within a few days.

Tangy Marinade

1 C. vegetable oil
½ C. vinegar
2 T. lemon juice
2 T. Finely chopped onion
1 clove garlic, minced
1 bay leaf
2 T. marjoram leaves
1 tsp. salt
1 tsp. pepper

Combine all ingredients in a medium mixing bowl, and mix well. Use marinade for steaks.

Yield about 2 cups.

Marinade for Pork Tenderloin

⅔ C. soy sauce (light is okay)
⅔ C. dry sherry
3 finely chopped garlic cloves
2 T. fresh ginger or 1 tsp. ground
dry mustard and thyme to taste

Rub tenderloin with dry mustard and thyme. Marinade 3-4 hours. Put in a zip lock bag. Turn over a couple of times. Bake on 375° for the first hour. Turn heat to 350°. Continue baking 45 minutes to 1 hour.

Manteiga De Molho
Butter Sauce

1 T. butter
1 tsp. minced parsley
1 tsp. lemon juice
salt and pepper

Cream butter. Add parsley, lemon juice, salt and pepper. Spread over hot broiled fish.

Basic Brown Sauce

¼ C. butter
¼ C. all-purpose flour
2 C. beef stock
⅛ tsp salt
⅛ tsp. Pepper

Melt butter in a medium saucepan. Add flour, blending well. Cook stirring constantly until mixture has browned.

Gradually add stock, cook over medium heat, stirring constantly, until thickened and bubbly. Stir in salt and pepper.

Serve sauce hot with roast beef or steak.

Yield about 2 C.

Molho Escuro
Brown Sauce

2 T. butter or fat
1 small onion
2 T. flour
1 C. beef or vegetable stock
½ tsp. Salt
¼ tsp. Pepper

Melt the butter or fat. Add the flour, let brown. Add liquid gradualy stirring constantly over lower heat. Season. Cook 5 minutes, stirring often. Serve as gravy with meat, or mashed potatoes.

Brown Mushroom Sauce

1 C. brown sauce
1 (6 oz. can) sliced mushrooms, 1 C. sauteed in butter.
1 tsp. chopped parsley

Make brown sauce using mushroom liquid and beef bouliion as liquid. Add mushrooms, heat and add fresh parsley.

Molho Picante
Hot Piquant Sauce

1 C. brown Sauce
½ small onion, chopped fine
2 T. lemon, vinegar, sherry or claret
1 T. each of capers and pickles, chopped and hot pepper to taste.

Make Brown Sauce, add remaining ingredients.

Serve hot with beef or pork.

Caper Sauce

Add ¼ C. of capers, drained, to 1 C. Brown Sauce.

Serve hot over burgers.

Capers Sauce

½ C. butter, divided
3 T. all-purpose flour
½ tsp. salt
⅛ tsp pepper
1½ C. hot water
1 tsp. Lemon juice
1 (3 oz.) jar capers, drained

Melt ¼ C. butter in a heavy saucepan over low heat. Add flour, salt, and pepper, stirring until smooth. Cook 1 minute, stirring constantly.

Gradually add water. Cook over medium heat, stirring constantly until thickened and bubbly. Gradually stir in lemon juice and remaining butter, heating constantly until butter is well blended. Add capers, stirring well.

Serve sauce warm over baked or broiled chicken or fish.

Yield 2 cups.

Café de Paris Sauce

16 oz. butter at room temp.
2 cloves of garlic, finely chopped.
2 T. onions grated
2 tsp. parsley
¼ tsp taragon
¼ tsp thyme
¼ tsp marjoran
1 tsp. worcestershire sauce
⅛ tsp. tabasco
salt and pepper to taste

With an electric mixer, blend everything together until fluffy. Line a cookie sheet with wax paper. Drop Cafe de Paris Sauce by the teaspoonful or use an icing bag to make dollops. Freeze in a sealed container. Serve over grilled steak or hamburger.

Molho Para Filetes
Sauce for Thin Steaks

1 clove of garlic
1 tsp. mustard
1 tsp. calda da pimenta or hot sauce
1 tsp. ketchup
1 T white or red wine
1 T. butter
salt and pepper to taste

Add all ingredients in a pot. Bring to a boil. Simmer for 5 minutes. Add water as needed.

Horseradish Sauce

1 C. whipping cream
2 T. prepared horseradish
1 T. taragon vinegar
½ tsp. salt
¼ tsp. pepper
1 tsp prepared mustard
¼ tsp. onion powdered
¼ tsp. Hot sauce

Beat whipping cream until just thickened. Add remaining ingredients, mixing well. Chill sauce at least 3 hours. Serve sauce cold with roast beef. Yield: about 2 cups.

Horseradish Mustard Sauce

1 C. mayonaise
2 T. prepared horseradish
2 T. horseradish mustard
2 ½ tsp. Sugar

Combine all ingredients. Mix well. Chill. Serve sauce with roast.

Horseradish and Sour Cream Sauce

½ C. prepared horseradish
½ C. sour cream
1 T. plus 1 tsp. vinegar
2 tsp. sugar
½ tsp. pepper

Combine all inredients. Stir well, cover and chill. Serve with roast. Yield 1 cup

Mushroom Sauce

½ sliced fresh mushrooms
1 T. butter
1 C. basic brown sauce
¼ C. sherry
1½ T. finely chopped green onion
⅛ tsp. Salt
⅛ tsp. Pepper

Saute mushrooms in butter until tender. Add Basic Brown Sauce, sherry, onion, salt, and pepper, stirring frequently.

Serve hot with roast beef or steak. Yield: about 1¼ C.

Mushroom Cream Sauce

2 lb. mushrooms
1 C. medium white sauce
1 tsp chopped parsley

Cut thin slices from mushroom stems and peel thinly if discolored. Wash. Remove stems and slice for sauce. Caps may be sauteed in a little butter and used to garnish the dish. Or use mushrooms whole, sliced or quartered.

Saute in a little butter. Make white sauce using mushroom liquid instead of part of water.

Add mushrooms and parsley and serve hot.

Mushroom Pan Gravy

½ C. sliced fresh mushrooms
2 T. butter
2 T. all-purpose white flour
1 C. beef broth
½ tsp. salt
⅛ tsp. pepper
dash of worstershire sauce
dash of ground nutmeg

Saute mushrooms in butter in a small saucepan over low heat, 5 minutes. Add flour, stirring until mushrooms are well coated. Cook 1 minute, stirring constantly. Gradually add beef broth, cook over medium heat, stirring constantly until thickened and bubbly. Stir in remaining ingredients.

Serve with hamburgers, meat loaf or steaks. Yield about ¾ C.

Roast Pan Gravy

¼ C. plus 2 T. butter
¼ C. plus 2 T. all-purpose flour
pan drippings from roast beef
water, salt and pepper to taste

Combine butter and flour in a heavy skillet. Stir until smooth. Cook stirring constantly, over medium heat until browned. Combine pan drippings and water to equal 3 C. Gradually add pan drippings mixture to skillet. Cook over medium heat stirring constantly until thickened and bubbly. Stir in salt and pepper.

Serve hot with roast beef or pork. Yield: about 3 cups

Rich Pan Gravy

3 T. pan drippings from roast beef
3 T. all-purpose flour
2 C. beef broth
¼ tsp. Pepper

Heat drippings in a heavy skillet over medium heat. Add flour, stir until smooth. Cook over low heat 2 minutes, stirring constantly until thickened. Stir in pepper. Serve hot.

Raison Sauce

1 C. brown sauce
12 C. seeded raisins
sherry or madeira to taste

Make brown sauce using any desired fruit juice as liquid. Add raisins, simmer 10 minutes. Add wine to taste and serve.

It's good with ham or pork.

Molho De Vinho
Wine Sauce

Heat ½ C. raisins with ¼ C. part wine. Combine with 1 C. whole cranberry sauce. Serve warm with meat or game.

Molho De Vilão

A little oil
Medium hot fresh pepper
garlic
A little wine
chopped green olives
salt

Add the wine or vinegar and chopped green olives. Serve over grilled or fried fish. Sprinkle with fresh parsley.

The word Vilão was used to describe a poor man.

Sweet and Sour Sauce

½ C. honey
½ C. prepared mustard
½ C. cider vinegar
¼ C. worcestershire sauce
2 tsp. hot sauce
1 tsp. salt
1 T. chopped fresh parsley

Combine all ingredients in a small saucepan. Stir well. Bring to a boil. Remove from heat.

Serve hot with broiled chicken. Yield: 1¾ C.

Lemon Sauce

juice of 1 lemon
¼ C. butter, softened
¼ tsp salt
⅛ tsp. pepper
1 egg yolk

Combine lemon juice, butter, salt and pepper in a small saucepan. Cook over medium heat, beating with a wire whisk until butter melts and all ingredients are well blended. Add a small amount of hot mixture to yolk, stir well, and add remaining hot mixture. Cook over low heat, beating well until mixture is smooth and slightly thickened.

Serve immediately with baked or broiled fish. Great with broiled chicken. Yield about ½ C.

Molho De Limão
Lemon Sauce

3 egg yolks
1 whole egg
juice of 2 lemons
2 C. fish stock
sugar to taste
¼ C. slivered almonds

Mix all ingredients. Place in double boiler. Beat well, cook until thick over boiling water (Bath Marie). Serve at once with poached or steamed fish.

Brown Egg Sauce

2 egg yolks, beaten
1 C. brown sauce (see below)
1 T. vinegar or lemon juice

Follow recipe for brown sauce,using fish liquid from poached fish. Stir the hot sauce gradually into the beaten youlks, stirring constantly until thick. Remove from heat and add vinegar or lemon juice.

Serve with fish.

Creamy Egg Sauce

6 hard cooked eggs diced
1 C. light cream
1 T. butter
salt and paprika
4 T. finely chopped parsley

Place the first 4 ingredients in top of double boiler. When thoroughly heated, add parsley and pour over cauliflour, asparagus or fish.

Spiced Port Wine Sauce

¾ C. port or other sweet red wine
1 T. sugar
1 tsp. whole cloves
1 stick cinnamon, broken in half
peel of 1 lemon
1 (12 oz.) far red currant jelly.

Combine wine, sugar, cloves cinnamon and lemon peel in a small saucepan. Bring to a boil, reduce heat, and simmer 15 minutes. Strain mixture, discarding spices and lemon peel. Return strained wine mixture to saucepan. Stir in jelly. Simmer 1 or 2 minutes, stirring occasionally.

Serve sauce warm with roast lamb. Yield: 1½ C.

Sour Cream and Chive Sauce

½ C. sour, cream
¼ mayonaise
1 T. minced shallots
1 T. chopped chives
1 T. fresh parsley
½ tsp. prepared mustard
½ tsp. Salt
⅛ tsp. pepper
⅛ tsp. Hot sauce
⅛ tsp. paprika

Combine sour cream, mayonaise, shallots, chives, parsley, mustard, salt, pepper and hot sauce with cold sliced roast lamb. Yield: about ¾ C.

Remoulade Sauce

2 C. mayonaise
2 hard boiled eggs, finely chopped
2 cloves garlic, crushed
1 T. drained capers
1 T. minced fresh parsley
½ tsp. dry mustard
½ tsp. dried tarragon leaves
½ tsp. Anchovy paste

Combine all ingredients in a mixing bowl. Stir well. Cover and refrigerate at least 3 hours. Serve sauce cold with poached fish or with chilled boiled shrimp.

Yield: 2½ cups.

Molho De Sardinhas
Sardine Sauce

4-6 small sardines
2 T. butter
2 T. flour
1 C. of fish or meat stock
Juice of ½ lemon
½ C. white wine
salt and pepper to taste
2 egg yolks

With a fork, mash the sardines. Melt butter, add flour, then the stock. Stir until smooth. Add lemon juice, wine and cook slowly for 10 minutes, season with salt and paepper to taste and stir in very gradually the egg yolks beaten with a little cold water.

Serve immedialtely with fish or meat.

Sour Cream Tartar Sauce

1 C. mayonaise
½ C. sour cream
2 T. finely chopped dill pickle
1 T. finely chopped onion
1 T. finely chopped fresh parsley
1 T. lemon juice
¼ tsp. Dried thyme
¼ tsp. Dried tarragon
⅛ tsp. Pepper

Combine all ingredients in a small mixing bowl, mixing well. Cover mixture, and chill overnight to blend flavors.

Serve sauce cold with fish or seafood. Yield: 1¼ cups.

Tartar Sauce

1 C. mayonaise
½ C. sweet pickle relish
¼ C. chopped onion (very fine)

Combine all ingredients in a small mixing bowl. Stir well, cover and chill at least 2 hours to blend flavors.

Serve sauce cold with fish or seafood.

Yield 1¼ cups

Snapper Sauce

2 lg. onions, finely chopped
2 cloves garlic, minced
1 green pepper, finely chopped
2 T. chopped fresh parsley
dash of dried whole thyme
1 T. butter, melted
1 T. all-purpose flour
1 (16 oz. can) tomatoes, chopped, undrained
¾ C. olives chopped

Saute first 5 ingredients in butter in a large skillet about 15 minutes over low heat.

Add flour and cook 1 minute, stirring constantly. Stir in tomatoes, simmer 10 minutes. Yield: about 2½ cups

Seafood Sauce

½ C. catsup
½ tsp. calder da pimenter
1 clove garlic
Medium white sauce

Rub inside of saucepan with garlic and make medium white sauce, using cream in place of milk.

When smooth, add rest of ingredients. Serve hot over lobster, shrimp, crab and oysters.

Dill and Mustard Sauce

2 to 2½ T. dry mustard
¼ C. plus 1 T. sugar
½ tsp. salt
2 T. vegetable oil
1 T. vinegar
½ C. commercial sour cream
2 T. fresh dill weed chopped

Combine mustard, sugar and salt. Mix well. Add oil and vinegar alternately, beating until well blended. Fold in sour cream and dill weed. Cover and chill thoroughly. Serve sauce cold with cold crab claws or other chilled shellfish.

Yield: 1 C.

Mint Sauce (#1)

1 C. sugar
½ C. vinegar
2 T. finely chopped, fresh mint leaves

Combine sugar and vinegar in a medium saucepan. Bring to a boil. Cook over high heat 5 minutes, stirring occasionally. Remove from heat, add mint leaves. Cover and let stand 5 minutes. Serve sauce hot with roast lamb. Yield: about ¾ C.

Molho De Ortelão
Mint Sauce (#2)

1½ T. sugar or ½ C. honey
½ C. cider vinegar
¼ C. chopped mint leaves (or more)

Dissolve sugar in vinegar. Pour over mint and let stand 30 minutes over low heat. If vinegar is strong, dilute with water to taste. Serve hot over hot lamb.

Tangy Mint Sauce (#3)

½ C. chili sauce
½ C. mint jelly
1 T. worcestershire sauce
1 T. prepared horseradish
2 tsp. prepared mustard
¼ pan dripping from roast of lamb

Combine all ingredients in a heavy saucepan. Bring to a boil. Reduce heat, simmer 10 minutes. Serve sauce hot with roast lamb. Yield: about 1½ C.

Molho Branco
Basic White Sauce

1 small onion, finely chopped
1 T. butter
1 T. all-purpose flour
1 C. milk
½ tsp. salt
⅛ tsp. White pepper

Saute onion in butter in a small saucepan over low heat until tender. Add flour. Stir well. Cook 1 minute, stirring constantly. Gradually add milk. Cook over low heat, stirring constantly until thickened and bubbly. Add salt and pepper. Stir well. Serve sauce hot with or as a base for other sauces. Yield: 1 cup.

My mother called this sauce as basic white sauce. The French call it Bechamel. It's the basic for many other sauces. Note: Warm milk eliminates lumps.

Molho Branco
White Sauce

1 C. hot milk
1 T. butter
1 T. flour
¼ tsp. salt
⅛ tsp. pepper

Cook as in Basic White Sauce.

Medium White Sauce

1 C. hot milk
2 T. buttered 3 T. flour
¼ tsp. salt
⅛ tsp. pepper

Scald milk. Set aside. Melt the butter in a saucepan over low heat or in a double boiler. Add flour, stirring constantly.

Stir in the hot milk gradually and cook, stirring constantly until the mixture thickens. If lumpy, beat well with a rotary beater. Season and serve hot.

Thick White Sauce

1 C. hot milk
3 T. butter
3 T. flour
¼ tsp salt.
⅛ tsp. Pepper

Scald milk. Melt the butter in a saucepan over low heat or in a double boiler. Add flour, stirring constantly. Stir in the hot milk gradually and cook stirring constantly until the mixture thickens. If lumpy, beat well with rotary beater. Season and serve hot.

Cream Sauce

1 C. hot medium white sauce with 2 egg yolks beaten into white sauce.

Cheese Sauce

Add ½ C. of grated chedder cheese to 1 C. hot medium white sauce or cream sauce

White Gravy

4 T. (½ stick butter)
5 T. all-purpose flour
1 C. milk
1 C. heavy cream or half and half
pinch of nutmeg
salt and freshly ground white peopper to taste

In a small saucepan, melt the butter, stir in the flour and cook 3 minutes.

Remove from heat and gradually blend warm milk and cream.

Heat to boiling, stirring constantly and cook until thickened, about 10 minutes.

Season with nutmeg, salt and pepper.

Also known as Bechamel saucepan.

Side Dishes

Glazed Fried Apples

4 medium apples, unpeeled and cored
¼ C. plus 2 T. butter
¼ C. sugar
¼ C. brown sugar, packed firm

Slice apples into ⅛ in. rings.

Place apples and butter in a large skilett Place apples and butter medium heat 10 minutes or until apples are tender.

Add sugar and cook uncovered 10 minutes or until golden brown.

Yield 6-8 servings.

Baked Fresh Asparagus

1½ lbs fresh asparagus spears, cleaned
dash of salt and pepper
3 T. olive oil
3 T. parmesan cheese

Drizzle the asparagus with olive oil. Place cleaned whole asparagus spears in a 12x8x2 inch baking dish. Sprinkle with salt, pepper and parmesan. Bake for 1 5 – 25 minutes in a pre-heated oven at 375° until asparagus is tender. Test for doneness.

Wrapped Asparagus Spears

6 asparagus, steamed
2 oz. Prosciutto, thinly sliced
1 garlic clove, minced
1 T. lemon juice
2 tsp. olive oil
parsley for garnish

Wrap asparagus spears with prosciuto. Sprinkle with garlic and drizzle with lemon and olive oil.

Serve with a slice of lemon and a sprig of parsley for an easy appetizer.

Toast Baskets

16 slices white bread, trimmed crust, lightly butter both sides.

Press each slice into an 8 oz. custard cup. Bake at 350° for 15 minutes or until lightly bowned. Remove cups. Cool completely on wire racks.

Yield 16 baskets. This is a great dinner appetizer.

Asparagus with Mushrooms & Cream Sauce

1 lb. large fresh mushrooms
¼ C. plus 1 T. butter divided
chopped fresh parsley
3 T. all-purpose flour
1 C. whipping cream
½ C. milk
¼ tsp. salt
¼ tsp. white pepper
2 lbs. fresh asparagus spears, cleaned and cooked
2 T. grated Parmesan cheese

Clean mushrooms with damp paper towels or mushroom brush.

Remove stems and chop. Saute mushroom caps and stems in 2 T. butter. Remove from heat and drain.

Fill each cap with parsley. Set stems and caps aside.

Melt remaining butter in a heavy saucepan over low heat. Add flour, stirring until smooth.

Cook 1 minute, stirring constantly. Gradually add whipping cream and milk. Cook over medium heat, stirring constantly, until mixture is thickened and bubbly. Add salt, pepper and reserved mushroom chopped stems.

Arrange cooked asparagus spears and mushrooms caps on an ovenfroof serving dish.

Pour sauce over asparagus. Sprinkle with cheese. Place uder broiler 2-3 minutes or until lightly brown. Yield: 6-8 servings.

In my house this dish is well-liked.

Creme De Feijão
Bean Puree

Parsley, butter, salt and pepper to taste
1 C. of sweet baby peas (fresh or frozen)
1 C. of beans, your favorites
1 lb. carrots
1 lb. turnips
3 T. olive oil

Cook beans without salt. When cooked, puree with water and olive oil, salt, pepper and butter.

Have carrots and turnips peeled and cut into small cubes. Add to the puree and cook for 10-15 minutes until vegetables are tender.

Serve with sprinkle of fresh chopped parsley.

Note: A short cut: use a can of beans (I prefer white.) Rinse and add water or stock, vegetable or chicken is good. Frozen baby sweet peas are just as good as fresh and can be used year round. Can be used as a side dish or as soup by adding more stock.

Broccoli Baked with Cheese Sauce

2½ lbs. fresh broccoli, cleaned and cooked
2 T. chopped onion
3 T. butter
3 T. all purpose flour
2½ C. milk
½ C. grated Parmesan cheese
½ tsp salt
½ tsp. dry mustard
¼ tsp. pepper
¼ tsp paprika
⅛ tsp. ground marjoram

¼ C. (1 oz.) shredded sharp chedder cheese for topping.

Place broccoli in a 12x8x2 inch baking dish. Saute onion in butter. Add flour, stirring until smooth. Cook 1 minute stirring constantly.

Gradually add milk. Cook over medium heat, stirring constantly until thickened and bubbly.

Add Parmesan chease, salt, mustard, pepper, paprika and marjoram. Stir until cheese melts. Spoon sauce over broccoli.

Bake at 375° for 15 minutes. Sprinkle chedder cheese over top. Bake 5 minutes.

Yield: 6-8 servings

Broccoli Parmesan

2½ lbs fresh broccoli, cleaned and cooked
½ tsp. salt
dash of pepper
2 T. butter
¾ C. parmesan cheese

Arrange broccoli in a serving dish. Season with salt and pepper. Pour melted butter over broccoli and sprinkle with parmesan cheese.

Place under broiler for 2 minutes or until cheese is golden brown.
Yield: About 8 serving

Fresh Brussels Sprouts

1 C. fresh mushrooms sliced
1 lb. fresh brussels sprouts
1 T. butter
2 T. lemon juice
3 strips bacon
½ small onion chopped
Parmesan cheese if desired

Cook the bacon in a skillet. Remove the bacon to a paper towel. Reserve the fat and saute onion and mushrooms. Set aside

Trim and wash the brussel sprouts. Add to a pot with water and salt. Bring to a boil and simmer for 10-15 minutes. Discard the water.

In the skillet crumble the bacon with onion and mushrooms. Add the brussel sprouts. Sprinkle the lemon, add butter and stir. Bring it back to warm and serve. Sprinkle with parmesan if desired.

Carraway Fettucine

⅓ C. milk
⅓ C. (chablis) or other dry white wine
1½ T. butter
3 C. cooked fettuccine (no salt or fat)
3 T. minced fresh parsley
2 tsp. caraway seeds
¼ tsp. salt
⅛ tsp. garlic powder

In a saucepan, combine milk, wine and butter.

On a medium heat, cook, stirring constantly until butter melts.

Add fettuccine and remaining ingredients. Cook tossing gently, until thoroughly heated.

Note: May substitute the wine by adding the juice of ½ lemon and a little more milk. It works well.

Carrot Fritters

1½ C. cleaned shredded carrots
3 C. soft breadcrumbs
½ C. milk
2 eggs, beaten
3 T. minced onion
¾ tsp. baking onion
¼ tsp. salt
⅛ tsp. pepper
vegetable oil
horseradish, optional

Combine first 8 ingredients. Mix well.

Heat 2 inches of oil in a heavy skillet over medium heat.

Drop mixture by tablespoonfuls into hot oil, 375°. Fry until golden brown, turning once. Drain.

Serve hot. Yield: 1 ½ dozen.

Serving suggestions: Carrot fritters may be served as an appetizer with horseradish sauce or as a side dish.

Puree De Cenaura
Carrot Puree

6 or 7 carrots
4 potatoes
1 cube of chicken or beef Knorr boullion
salt and pepper and butter to taste
croutons

Cook the carrots, potatoes and onions. Cut into pieces. When cooked, puree. Add salt, pepper, butter and Knorr. Stir well.

Serve with fresh small croutons done in butter.

Baked Cauliflower

1 medium head of cauliflower cleaned and cooked
⅓ C. fine dry breadcrumbs
⅓ C. butter melted
1 tsp. salt
parmesan cheese for topping

Cauliflower should be soaked 20 mintes head down.

Add salt and water. Bring to a boil. Remove cauliflower, place in a 3 qt. casserole. Sprinkle with breadcrumbs and bake uncovered at 350 for 20 minutes.

Yield: 6 servings

Transfer to a serving dish. Sprinkle with Parmesan cheese.

Dumplings

6 Kaiser rolls
5 oz. butter
½ onion, chopped very fine
1 T. or more fresh parsley, chopped
⅜ C. milk (more if needed)
3 eggs

Day old bread is better. Cut bread unto small cubes. Add ingedients together. Let stand for 1 hour. If a little dry, add more milk.

Use cheese cloth or a large napkin.

Form the mixture into a log roll and tie the napkin or cheese cloth ends. (If the log is too long, use a tooth pick in the middle)

In a large pot of water, add salt. Bring to a boil. Add dumplings and simmer for 45 minutes.

Great to serve with pork or beef. Add a light sauce.

I make more than needed. The next day, fry with a pat of butter and serve with eggs for breakfast. Excellent!

Split Green Beans

3 lbs. fresh green beans
Pinch of baking soda
2 T. butter
1½ tsp. salt
¼ tsp. pepper
½ C. slivered almonds

Break tips from beans, remove strings if necessary. Wash in cold water and drain. Using a knife, cut each bean lengthwise into several slices.

Place beans, soda, and water to cover in a medium saucepan. Bring to a boil and cook 2 minutes. Drain well.

Return beans to saucepan. Add water to cover and bring to a boil. Reduce heat, cover and simmer 10 minutes until tender or to taste.

Drain. Add butter, salt and pepper, stirring well. Sprinkle almonds over beans to serve.

Yield: 8 servings.

Mushroom Casserole

Butter a 2 qt. casserole.

Butter 3 slices of stale bread. Cube and put in casserole.

Saute 1 lb. of sliced mushrooms in butter about 5 minutes.

Add ½ C. each chopped onion, green pepper and mayonaise. Add ¾ tsp. salt and pepper. Stir mixture and cook a little longer.

Then spread over cubed buttered bread.

Beat together 1 ½ C. milk and 2 eggs. Pour over all and chill at least 1 hour or overnight.

Remove from refrigerater and spread undiluted can of mushroom soup over all.

Add crushed cracker crumbs, buttered and crumbled. Spread over all. If desired, ½ C. grated cheese may be added. I do.

Serves 10-12. Can be made ahead and re-heated.

Market list:
3 slices thick bread
¾ tsp. pepper and salt
1 lb. mushrooms
1¼ C. milk
1 C. onions
2 eggs
1 C. peppers
1 C. crumbled crackers
Butter as needed for crackers and bread
½ C. grated cheese

Ervilhas

Põe-se agua ao lume ja com os temperos. Quando ferver deitam-se batata partida aos quadradinhas e as ervilhas. Deixa-se cozer e serve-se.

Peas

Put the water on the flame with the spices. When it comes to a boil, add potatoes cut into small cubes and peas. Let it cook and serve.

One of the many examples how recipes were written in past recipe books.

Potatoes

Last summer my brother and family came to visit. One night during dinner, the conversation turned to "remember when?"

My brother started to tell stories about when we were children.

One such story he reminded me of was, how much I liked new little white potatoes.

In our house, dinner was full of conversation as is in mine now.. I was quite good at dominationg the subject. That night, I was in my glory. He didn't remember what else we had for dinner, but one of the things was my very favorite. New little potatoes, the first of the season.

I was eating everything else and leaving the mouth watering delicious little potatoes cut in half, skin on, cooked in salted water with 1 or 2 garlic cloves, drained of the water and finished with fresh, flat chopped parsley.

As usual, I was talking a lot. My father kept on stealing my potatoes from my plate one at a time. I never noticed. Everyone was in on the joke, including my mother. She removed the serving dish and I missed that as well.

When I looked at my plate, only one half of such a little potato was left on the plate. They couldn't stop laughing. The more I asked, "What's so funny?", the more they laughed until my mother brought back the potatoes.

My brother Manuel, as he was telling the story, laughed as much as he did that day, so I finished the story for him.

I must confess, I still love potatoes of all kinds prepared in many ways. So during the writing of this book, there was no question that potato dishes would be included.

Potato Pancakes

3 large potatoes (1 ½ lbs.)
1 medium size onion grated
½ tsp. freshly grond black pepper
1 T. all-purpose flour
¼ tsp. baking powder
2 eggs, seperated
½ C. vegetable oil

Peel and grate potatoes into a sieve. With the back of a wooden spoon, press out the excess moisture.

In a medium size bowl, combine the potato, onion, salt, pepper, flour and baking powder. Toss to mix.

Lightly beat the egg yolks and stir into potato mixture.

Beat the egg whites until stiff, but not dry and fold into potato mixture.

Heat oil in a heavy skillet. Drop batter by serving spoonfuls into hot oil so that they do not touch. Cook over medium heat until golden, turn and brown the other side. Drain on paper towels and repeat until all batter is used, keeping the cooked pancakes warm.

Seve with unsweetened applesauce.

Note: These pancakes are a brunch time favorite in my home.

Molho Verde Com Batatas
Potatoes With Green Sauce

⅓ C. olive or vegetable oil
1 large onion, finely chopped (1 C.)
2 cloves garlic, finely chopped
3 lbs. boiled potatoes, peeled and sliced or if red skinned, scrubbed and skins left on
1 C. finely shredded fresh spinach
¼ C. finely chopped fresh parsley
1½ tsp. Salt
½ tsp. freshly ground pepper

In a heavy saucepan, heat the oil and saute the onion until tender but not browned. Add the garlic and cook, stirring 3 mintes. Add potato slices and enough hot water to barely cover.

Bring to a boil, cover, and cook slowly 15 minutes, or until potato is barely tender but holds it's shape.

Add spinach, parsley, salt and pepper and re-heat. Serve in bowls with cooking liquid.

Pie De Batatas
Potato Pie

3 T. buttered 6 medium size yellow onions, thinly sliced
1 clove garlic, finely chopped
4 lbs red-skinned potatoes, peeled and thinly sliced
2 tsp. salt
½ tsp. freshly ground black pepper
⅓ C. flour
1½ C. milk
Pastry for a double crust 9-inch pie
1 C. heavy cream.

Heat the butter in a skillet and saute the onion until tender but not browned. Add the garlic and cook 5 minutes.

Place the potato slices in a large saucepan. Cover with boiling salted water and cook 3 minutes. Drain.

Butter a shallow 3 qt. casserole and alternate layers of onion and potato, sprinkling each layer with some of the salt and pepper. Preheat oven to 350°.

Place the flour in a small bowl and gradually stir in the milk. Pour over casserole. Roll out pastry to fit top of casserole. Decorate the edge and make a large round hole in the middle to allow steam to escape. Brush pastry with some of the cream.

Bake at 350° for 1 hour, or until pastry is golden brown. Heat cream and pour into hole.

Let stand 10 minutes before serving.

Pure De Batata Ricas
Mashed Potatoes for Company

8-10 potatoes, cooked and mashed
1 8 oz. pkg cream cheese
1 tsp salt
1 C. sour cream

Mix all ingredients together until smooth. Place in a shallow baking dish and add several pats of butter to top. Sprinkle with paprika.

Bake at 200° 1½ to 2 hours or at 350° for 45 minutes.

Excellent way to do potatoes ahead of time. Can be refrigerated up to 24 hours before baking.

Batatas Esmagadas
Smashed Potatoes

5 medium size potatoes
3 T. grated cheese
3 tsp. of extra virgin olive oil
1 C. milk
2 oz. Butter
salt and pepper to tast
3 slices bacon

Serves 4 abundant servings.

Wash potatoes and put in a pot with cold water to cover the potatoes well. Add salt and cook, 25 to 30 minutes.

While potatoes are cooking, heat traditional 3 spoons of olive oil and bring to heat. Add paprika to give color and taste. Next add cooked bacon. Let the bacon cook for 3 minutes or until bacon is crispy. Turn off the heat.

Test the potatoes by inserting a knife. When the blade goes easily in, it means the cooking is done.

Remove the water from the pot and peel each potato. Mash the potatoes, then add milk and bring to a boil. If needs, may add a little more milk. Pour the smashed potatoes into a bowl. Add 3 T. of grated cheese or your favorite. Add the bacon with its grease.

Mix everythig together. Adjust salt and pepper to taste and the dish is ready to serve.

"Some add chopped tomato and a bunch of black grapes to the sauce."

Note: you may cover the dish with aluminum foil and keep it in the oven on warm.

Repolho Vermelho
Red Cabbage

1 red cabbage, sliced very fine
1 yellow onion, chopped
5 T. vinegar
3 T. water
4 geen apples peeled and chopped
1 tsp. salt
¼ tsp pepper
1 tsp. sugar

In a heavy pot, add all the ingredients. Cook very slowly with lid on for a couple of hours until cabbage is tender and apples have melted into it.

Adjust vinegar to your taste.

Good to serve with pork dishes.

Will keep in fridge in a glass jar for over a month. Served cold is just as good.

Sebola Vermelho Com Azeitonas
Red Onion and Olive Tart

9 oz. puff pastry
1 egg, lightly beaten
2 T. olive oil
3-4 red onions
salt to taste and ground pepper.
4 egg yolks
1 ¼ C. heavy whipping cream
1 T. chopped thyme (may use dried)
¾ C. black olives, pitted, thyme to garnish.

Use a 9 inch springform tart pan. Roll out the pastry on a lightly floured surface an line the tin.

Brush the base with beaten egg and prick the base all over with a fork.

Bake in a heated oven at 425° for 12 minutes. Remove from oven.

Press the pastry base down with your fingers. Reduce the oven temperature to 350°.

Heat the skillet and gently cook the onions until just softened, season to taste with salt and pepper and set aside to cool.

Beat together the egg yolks, cream and thyme. Stir into the onions and pour into the pastry pan. Bake for about 30 minutes until the filling is just set and lightly browned.

Scatter with olives for the last 10 minutes of baking.

Remove the sides of the tin and leave to stand for 10 minutes before serving. Sprinkle with thyme to garnish.

Serve with a green salad at lunch or a light dinner.

Arroz Verde
Green Rice

1 T. olive oil
1 large (medium heat) pepper, chopped
½ C. chopped white onion
½ tsp. cumin
½ C. fresh flat leaf parsley
1 tsp. salt
½ tsp. black pepper
1 C. black olives chopped or cut in half
4 C. water
5 oz. baby spinach
1-2 oz. crumbled queso fresco (a good substitute is mexican cheese.)
Olive oil drizzed over all

In a skillet over medium heat, add pepper and onion. Cook stirring occasionaly until tender, about 8 minutes, add garlic and cumin. Cook stirring until fragrant, one minute. Transfer mixture to a food processor and add parsley, salt pepper and olive oil.

Meanwhile, place 4 C. water in a large microwavable bowl, and microwave on medium high until hot about 4-5 minutes. Add baby spinach, let stand 1 minutes.

Remove spinach, squeeze between paper towels to remove excess moisture. Add spinach to mixture in food processor.

Process until smooth, about 45 seconds stopping to scrape sides as needed.

Cook rice to package directions. Transfer hot rice to a large bowl an stir in parsley mixture.

Tap with queijo fresco mexican cheese.

Serve immediately. Sprinkle last 2-3 T. our rice.

Green Rice Casserole

¼ C. (½ stick) butter
1 onion chopped,(1 C.)
3 C. cooked rice (1 C. raw)
2 C. (8 oz.) shredded sharp chedder
1 C. chopped fresh parsley
½ tsp. salt
¼ tsp freshly ground black pepper
2 eggs, lightly beaten
2 C. milk

In a small skillet heat the butter and saute the onion until tender but not browned. Preheat oven to 350°. In a greased casserole, combine the rice, cheese, parsley, salt, pepper, and cooked onion mixture. Toss to mix, combine the eggs and milk, pour over rice.

Bake at 350° for 45 minutes or until set.

The green rice compliments steamed or broiled fish.

Curried Rice

20 to 24 oz. chicken broth
3 C. uncooked regular rice
1½ tsp. curry powdered
1 tsp. salt

Bring chicken broth to boil in a medium saucepan.

Add rice and seasoning, reduce heat to low.

Cover and simmer 20 minutes or until tender.

Serve hot. Yield 6 Cups.

Breding Stuffing

4 oz. extra vrigin olive oil
2 ½ C. bread crumbs (fresh)
½ C. grated cheese (your choice)
2 cloves garlic, mashed
salt and pepper to taste

Pour the garlic grated cheese and bread crumbs in a mixing bowl.

Add olive oil. Adjust with salt and pepper.

Mix everything with your hand so that you understand if mixture is too dry, may add a little milk if needed.

Your breading is ready to be formed into round fritters.

In a skillet, add a little oil, fry on both sides until golden brown.

Serve as a side dish.

Ananas De Forno
Baked Pineapple

1 large can crushed pineapple in its own juice
1 egg
1 T. sugar
¼ C. flour
1 stick of butter
plain breadcrumbs
Pam spray

Spray a casserole with Pam.

Beat the egg, then add crushed pineapple, flour, and sugar. Mix well.

Put pats of butter over entire top of mixture.

Sprinkle well with breadcrumbs. Bake at 350° for 30-45 minutes. Good with ham or pork.

Originaly fresh pineapple was used. I find canned crushed or cubed is fine.

Apple Glazed Sweet Potatoes

2½ C. unsweetened 100% apple juice
½ tsp. ground cinamon
¼ tsp. salt
2 lbs. sweet potatoes (about 4 small potatoes) peeled and thinly sliced.

Combine apple juice, cinnamon, and salt in a large skillet. Add sliced sweet potatoes.

Reduce heat slightly and simmer potatoes, stirring occasionaly for 20-25 minutes or until potatoes are tender and juice has been reduced to a glaze.

Serve while hot. Serves 4. Season to taste.

Glazed Sweet Potatoes

6 medium size sweet potatoes
½ C. honey
¼ C. orange juice
¼ C. butter
2 T. lemon juice

Combine sweet potatoes and water and cover in a large dutch oven.

Reduce heat. Cover and simmer 30 minutes or until tender.

Drain, peel, slice potatoes lengthwise into ¼ inch thick slices.

Place potatoes in a large skillet and set aside.

Combine remaining ingredients in a small saucepan. Bring to a boil and stir until butter melts.

Remove from heat, pour honey, and cook uncovered over medium heat 20 minutes, basting often with honey mixture.

Transfer potatoes to a warm serving platter. Serve immediately.

Yield: 6 servings.

Sweet Potatoes and Pineapple

6 sweet potatoes cooked, cooled and sliced
6 slices of pineapple cut in pieces or crushed
⅔ C. pineapple juice
¼ C. butter
½ C. brown sugar

In a casserole, alternate layers of potatoes and pineapple. Pour the juice, butter and sugar mixture over top.

Bake 30 minutes at 350°. Serve with roast pork.

Recheadas De Tomate
Tomatoes with Dressing

4 large tomatoes cut in half (I prefer medium)
4 (10 oz.) packages frozen chopped spinach
1 C. soft bread crumbs
1 C. seasoned bread crumbs
1 C. finely chopped green onions
6 eggs slightly beaten
¾ C. butter melted
½ C. grated parmesan cheese
1 tsp. Thyme
¾ tsp. Salt
½ tsp minced garlic

Place the halved tomatoes, seeds and center removed, in a lightly greased 13x9 inch baking dish. Set aside.

Squeeze excess water from cooked spinach and combine with remaining ingredients. Mound mixture on tomatoes.

Bake at 350° for 25 minutes or until spinach mixture is set.

Note: Left over is good the next day by reheating in microwave.

Arroz De Legumes
Vegetable Rice

1 onion chopped fine
3 large carrots cut into small cubes
1 C. peas, fresh or frozen swet baby peas
1 C. rice uncooked
1 T. olive oil
1 T. butter
1 T. tomato paste and ¾ C. water
1 tsp. chicken base (Jones)
salt and pepper to taste
About 1 more cup of water or more to add while cooking

Saute onion, carrots, rice and olive oil about 10 minutes on medium heat. Stir often.

Add peas, chicken base and tomato paste.

Keep adding water as needed until the rice and vegetables are cooked. The rice should be a bit wet, but not runny. Keep adding water as it is cooking.

Baked Zucchini Fans

3 T. chopped onions
2 small cloves garlic, crushed
¼ C. olive oil, divided
3 T. breadcrumbs
12 small zucchini
¼ C. grated Parmesan cheese

Saute onion and garlic in 2 T. olive oil until tender. Remove from heat. Stir in breadcrumbs. Set aside.

Cut each zucchini into 4 lengthwise slices leaving slices atached on stem end.

Fan slices out and place in 15x10x1inch jellyroll pan. Brush zucchini fans lightly with remaining 2 T. olive oil.

Sprinkle each fan lightlywith ½ tsp breadcrumbs mixture and 1 tsp. Parmesan cheese.

Bake at 350° for 15-20 minutes or until crisp and tender.

Serves 12. It's good and looks good as well.

Zesty Zucchini Saute

1¼ lbs zucchini (about 3 medium zucchini)
1½ T. olive oil
1 T. dried oregano
2 cloves garlic, finely chopped
1 tsp. grated lemon peel
1 T. grated parmesan cheese
¼ tsp. ground black pepper

Cut zucchini in half crosswise. Cut each half into 4 lengthwise sticks.

Heat oil in a heavy non stick skillet over medium heat.

Add oregano and garlic and saute for about 3 minutes.

Add zucchini and lemon peel and saute fo about 3 minutes or until zucchini is lightly browned.

Mix parmesan cheese and pepper. Taste for flavor, adjust if needed.
Serves 4

Soups

Soup is a tradition goes back to the earliest days of civilized man, from the advent of fire. Soup remains a favorite and has become a special treat, especially on a cold winters day.

My father loved eating soups of all kinds. For him a meal was not a meal if it did not start with soup. Everyday my mom made a soup, the type of soup depending on the time of year. Soup could be the starter or the main dish at the end of the day.

Now, when I hear famous chefs say their specialty is cooking from farm to table, it makes me smile. Yes, a new concept. Back to the beginning we go.

Sopa Cove De Flôr
Cauliflower Soup

½ C. chopped onion
1 T. butter
1½ qts chicken broth, divided
1½ C. cooked regular rice
1 medium head cauliflower, shredded or riced
1 C. heavy cream
1 tsp. salt to taste
½ tsp pepper to taste
Curry powder, optional

Saute onion in butter in a medium size pan until tender. Add 3 C. chicken broth. Bring to a boil. Reduce heat, simmer uncovered 15 minutes.

Remove from heat, stir in rice.

Pour rice mixture into container of an electric blender and process until smooth.

Combine chestnuts and remaining chicken broth. Bring to a boil. Reduce heat, simmer uncovered 15 minutes or until tender.

Reduce heat, cover and simmer 1 hour or until chestnuts are tender. Place chestnut mixture in container of a blender. Process on high speed until smooth..

Stir in rice mixture, cream, salt and pepper and serve.

I also like to add ½ tsp of curry powder with the salt and pepper

Sopa De Castanhas
Cream of Chestnut Soup

1 ½ lbs. chestnuts
3 C. chicken broth
2 T. butter
2 T. all-purpose flour
3 C. milk
½ tsp. Salt
¼ tsp pepper
chopped fresh parsley

Place Chestnuts and water to cover in a small butch oven. Bring to a boil.

Cover and cook 20 minutes. Remove from heat. drain and cool. Remove shells from chestnuts and peel. Coarsely chop chestnuts. Combine chestnuts and chicken broth in a medium saucepan. Place over medium heat and bring to a boil.

Reduce heat, cover and simmer one hour or until chestnuts are tender.

Place chestnuts mixture in container of an electric blender. Process on high speed until smooth. Melt butter in a large sauce pan over low heat. Add flour, stirring until smooth.

Cook 1 minute, stirring constantly. Gradually add milk and cook over medium heat, stirring constantly until mixture is bubbly and begins to thicken. Remove from heat.

Add pureed chestnut mixture, salt and pepper to cream sauce, beating with a wire whisk. Place over low heat. Cook, stirring constantly until thoroughly heated.

Ladle soup into individual serving bowls. Garnish with chopped parsley and serve. Yield about 1 qt.

Sopa De Galinha Con Milho
Chicken and Corn Soup

1 (3½ lb.) broiler fryer cut up.
2 cups water
1 medium onion , chopped
¼ C. chopped fresh parsley
1 tsp. Salt
1 tsp. white pepper
1 small bay leaf
6 ears fresh yellow corn, cleaned, and kernals cut from cob (a good substitute is frozen corn)
1 C. uncooked egg noodles
Chopped hard boiled egg

Combine chicken, water, onion, parsley, salt, pepper, and bay leaf in a large pot. Bring to a boil. Reduce heat. Cover and simmer 45 minutes or until chicken is tender.

Remove chicken from broth, cool, bone chicken and cut meat into bite size pieces. Set aside.

Add corn to chicken broth. Simmer uncovered 20 minutes, stirring frequently. Stir in noodles and simmer an additional 10 minutes stirring frequently. Remove and discard bay leaf. Stir in chicken and cook until heated.

Serve garnished with chopped hard boiled egg.

Crab Soup for Company

2 cans pepperpot soup (Campbell's)
2 cans tomato soup
2 cans old fashioned vegetable soup (no beef)
6 cans water
1 lb. crabmeat
8 oz bag frozen mixed vegetables
1 stick cinnamon
1 T. parsley (to taste)

Combine and bring to boil. Simmer 1 hour

Serves 12-15

Note: freezes well. Don't tell them it's from the pantry to the pot. Surprise!

Sopa De Paixe
Fish Soup

2 C. water
1 C. peeled, diced potatoes
1 C. chopped celery
1 C. chopped carrots
2½ tsp. salt, divided
1 medium thinly sliced onion
2 T. butter
1 lb. fish, trout or fresh cod is best, raw or cooked, your choice, cut into 1-inch pieces
1 tsp. calda da pimenta
¼ tsp. white pepper
2 C. milk
2 T. all-purpose flour
paprika and chopped parsley

Combine water, potatoes, carrots, celery, ½ tsp. of salt in a medium saucepan. Bring to a boil. Reduce heat. Cover and simmer 15 minutes. Set aside. Saute onion in butter in a large Dutch oven until tender.

Add fish and calda da pimenta. Cook over medium heat 1 minute stirring gently Add cooked vegetables and liquid, remaining salt, and pepper. Cover and simmer.

Gradually stir milk into flour until smooth.

Stir milk mixture into fish. Cover over low heat 15 minutes or until thoroughly heated.

Serve in individual bowls. Sprinkle parsley and paprika on soup.

Sopa De Feijão Con Couve

How this soup got a new name: "Good for You Soup."

When my son Eric was a young child, he didn't care for this soup. Everytime I served it to him, he would say, "Mom, I really don't like this soup."

My answer was always the same. "Eat it; it's good for you."

It went on for years. One day, he must have been in sixth or seventh grade, he came home from school hungry as always as boys that age are. As he walked through the kitchen, he asked, "What are you cooking?"

As he lifted the lid from the pot on the stove, he exclaimed, "Oh! The Good for You Soup."

Again, I had a good laugh and as of that day, the soup became the "Good for You Soup."

Sopa De Feijão Con Couve
Greens with Red Bean Soup

1 onion chopped
4 or 5 large leaves of greens chopped (stems removed)
1 C. red beans, dried
4 carrots chopped into small pieces
4 potatoes or use 1 C. uncooked macaroni
2 T. olive oil
2 T. vegetable oil
1 T. vinegar
½ lemon juice
8-9 C. water
salt and pepper to taste
¼ to ½ tsp. red pepper flakes (may omit)

The night before, wash beans. Add beans and water and bring to boil. Remove from heat and let it soak overight.

When ready to make the soup, dispose of the water and return the beans to the pot and 1 C. of beans mashed. It gives body to the soup.

Next, add the chopped greens, carrots and potatoes. When cooked, add the juice of ½ lemon. Adjust flavors and serve. Note. Some times I replace the cup of beans with 2 cans of red beans. It's faster and just as good.

This soup freezes well with the macaroni as a substitute for the potatoes.

Caldo Verde
Green Soup

8 C. water
6 medium potatoes
3 cloves garlic
10 large leaves of greens (We call this type kale.)
Chaurico or 2 Italian sausages for flavor cut into slices
2 T. olive oil

In a pot, add water, salt, olive oil. Bring to a boil and add greens and chouriço. Cook for about 20 minutes on medium heat. Add potatoes, peeled, and cut into cubes. Continue cooking in a low temerature until tender. Cook without the lid on to keep the color. Serve with a slice of country bread.

Note: A good substitute for Chaurico is Mexican sausage.

Açorda De Otrelão
Mint Soup

6 C. water
2 cloves of garlic cut in half
½ tsp salt
3 T. olive oil or vegetable oil
1 or 2 small sprigs of mint
4 eggs, at room temp.
Bread, hard crust - 1 french baguette, stale is ok

Bring water to a boil, add mint, salt, oil and garlic. Cover the pot and let it stand 15 minutes.

Cut the bread into cubes (bite size). Beat eggs.

Remove the mint leaves and garlic.

Add the beaten eggs to the broth and stir, bring it back to a boil and add the bread.

Remove from the heat and serve. If you like, cut a few mint leaves and add to top of soup.

This soup was the favorite of my grandmother and her sister Rosa who served this soup mostly in the spring and summer. As one or the other would say, "Nice, light and refreshing." Outside their back door they had a pot on a stand growing mint.

I once asked grandmother, "Why not in the garden?"

"Ah! This way the mint can't walk." She added, "Mint is an invasive plant."

Serves 4

Mushroom and Barley Soup

1 medium onion, chopped
¼ C. butter
3 carrots peeled and chopped
1 C. diced clery
3 potatoes, peeled and diced
1 lb. fresh mushrooms sliced.
½ C. barley
2 T. chopped fresh parsley
22 oz. beef broth
1 tsp. Salt

Saute onion in butter in a large Dutch oven until tender.

Add remaining ingredients, stirring well.

Cover and simmer 1½ hours or until vegetables and barley are tender.

Serve chowder hot in individual bowls.

Yield: About 2 qts.

Sopa Do Norte
Northern Soup

6 medium potatoes, peeled and sliced
6 tomatoes, peeled and coarsely chopped
1 medium onion, thinly sliced
1 turnip, peeled and diced
2 large carrots, sliced
2½ C. frozen green peas
¼ C. uncooked regular rice
1 T. salt
½ tsp. pepper
1 tsp. sugar
dash of ground allspice
2 qts. beef broth (or vegtable)

Layer potatoes, tomatoes, onion, turnip, carrots, peas and rice in a 5 qt. casserole. Sprinkle sugar, salt, pepper, and allspice over vegetables.

Pour broth over vegetables.

Cover tightly and bake at 300° for 5 hours.

Remove from oven and ladle into individual serving bowls. Serve hot.

Yield about 5 qts.

Outra Sopa De Batata
Cream of Potato and Leek Soup

6 large potatoes
2 celery ribs
3 leeks (white part only)
1 small onion
6 C. chicken broth
½ tsp. pepper
½ tsp marjoram
½ tsp. basil
16 oz. heavy whipping cream
1 T. cornstarch
chopped chives

Combine chicken broth and vegetables. Bring to a boil, reduce heat, cover and simmer until vegetables are tender.

Using an immersion blender, puree the soup until smooth.

Return to heat and add pepper, marjoram, basil, salt and cornstarch if needed.

Simmer 5 minutes and add cream.

Ladle soup into individual serving bowls and garnish with chopped chives. Serve warm.

Sopa De Batata
Potato Soup

6 medium potatoes, peeled and cubed
1 large onion, chopped or exchange for leeks
½ C. diced green pepper
3 C. chicken broth
1½ C. milk
½ C. half and half
3 stalks celery
1 tsp. Salt
¼ tsp. white pepper
3 T. butter
dash of red pepper flakes and paprika
fresh parsley, chopped

Combine potatoes, onion or leeks, celery and green pepper in a pot with 3 C. chicken broth. Bring to a boil. Reduce heat, cover and simmer 25 minutes or until potatoes are tender.

Place vegetables and enough cooking liquid in container of an electric blender to blend smoothly. Process until smooth.

In one cup of cooking broth, combine pureed vegetables mixture and next 6 ingredients. Reserve half parsley mixing well.

Cook stirring constantly until soup is thoroughly heated. Do not boil.

Serve with chopped parsley on top.

Sopa De Abobara
Pumpkin Soup

1 can white beans (15 oz.) rinsed and drained
1 small onion or 2 tsp. onion powder.
1 C. water
1 can plain pumpkin (15 oz.) - saves time
1 can chicken or vegetable both (14.5 oz.)
½ tsp. thyme or tarragon
salt and pepper optional to taste

Easy prep.

Blend white beans and water. In a soup pot, mix beans. Puree with pumpkin, broth and spices. Cover and cook over low heat about 15–20 minutes until warmed through. Sprinkle chives or parmesan cheese.

Serve with a slice of good bread.

Note: It's a good go-to meal for a busy day.

Cream of Shrimp Soup

2 lbs. uncooked medium shrimp peeled, deveined, and halved
½ C. butter
¼ tsp. garlic powder.
¼ C. plus 2 T. all-purpose flour
3 C. whipping cream
3 C. chicken broth
1 bay leaf
1½ tsp. salt
½ tsp. white pepper
2 T. chopped chives

Saute shrimp in butter and garlic powder in a Dutch oven 5 minutes; remove shrimp with a slotted spoon and set aside.

Reserve pan dripping. Add flour to pan drippings. Stir until smooth. Cook 1 minute, stirring constantly.

Gradually add whipping cream, broth and bay leaf. Cook over medium heat stirring constantly until thickened and bubbly.

Stir in salt, pepper and chives. Remove and discard bay leaf.

Ladle soup into individual serving bowls. Serve warm.

Yield 2 qts.

Shrimp Soup

1 C. chopped celery
½ C. diced onion
2 small cloves garlic, minced
3 T. butter
2 T. olive oil
1 qt. water
2 (14½ oz.) cans whole tomatoes, undrained and chopped
1 C. catsup
¼ tsp. hot sauce
1 T. salt
1 tsp. celery seeds
¼ tsp. pepper
2 lbs uncooked medium shrimp, peeled and deveined
1 T. lemon juice
½ C. cracker crumbs
hot cooked rice.

Saute celery, onion, and garlic in butter in a small Dutch oven until tender. Stir in next 9 ingredients. Bring to a boil. Reduce heat, cover and simmer 30 minutes, stirring occasionally.

Return to a boil, stir in shrimp and lemon juice. Reduce heat to medium, cook 5 minutes, stirring occasionaly. Stir in cracker crumbs.

Spoon shimp mixture over hot cooked rice in individual serving bowls. Serve immediately. Yield: about 1 gallon

Sopa De Verão
Summer Soup

3 C. water
1 C. peeled diced potatoes
1 C. peeled sliced carrots
2½ tsp. salt
1 (16 oz.) frozen green peas, originally used fresh
1 C. fresh cauliflower florets
1 C. fresh broccoli
3 T. butter
3 T. all-purpose flour
3 C. milk
¼ tsp. white pepper
Chopped fresh parsley

Combine water, potatoes, carrots and salt in a large pot. Bring to a boil.

Reduce heat, cover and simmer 10 minutes. Stir in peas, cauliflower and broccoli. Cover and simmer an additional 10 minutes or until vegetables are tender.

Melt butter in a small pot over low heat. Add flour, stirring until smooth. Cook 1 minute stirring constantly. Gradually add milk and cook over medium heat until thickened and bubbly.

Stir into the vegetables; add pepper. Cook uncovred until it is hot. Adjust for salt and pepper.

Ladle soup into bowls. Sprinkle with parsley and serve.

Sopa Para O Jantar
One Dish Supper Soup

1 C. chopped celery
2 small onions, chopped
1 green pepper, seeded and chopped
1 T. butter
3 C. boiling water
2 C. chopped peeled tomatoes
½ tsp salt
6 eggs
Salt and pepper to taste
1 C. (8 oz.) shredded sharp chedder
hot cooked rice

Saute celery, onion, and green pepper in butter in a 4 qt. Dutch oven until tender.

Stir in boiling water, tomatoes and salt, mix well. Simmer, uncovered 15 minutes. Carefully break eggs into hot soup. Do not stir. Add salt and pepper. Sprinkle cheese over egg and soup mixture.

Cover and simmer 5 minutes. Serve immediately over rice in individual soup bowls soup bowls.

Yield: six serving

Tortelini Soup Stew

1 large can tomatoes
1 lb. Italian sweet sausages cut in pieces (don't brown)
1 15 oz. Hunts tomato sauce
4-7 C. beef stock
1 cut chopped onions
2 cloves garlic minced
1 C. sliced carrots
1 tsp. dry basil
1 tsp. oregano
2 C. sliced zucchini
1 C. sliced fresh mushrooms
2 to 4 C. fresh frozen tortelini (your choice)

Combine tomatoes, sausage, tomato sauce, beef stock, onion, garlic, carrots, basil, and oregano in a large pot. Simmer 30 minutes. Do not boil. Add remaining ingredients and simmer another 30 minutes.

Add tortellini last and cook for about 10 minutes

Serve with a good Italian bread. It's a good substitute for Portuguese house bread. Its a meal in a bowl.

I like cheese-filled Tortellini.

Sopa De Legumes
Vegetable Soup

1 onion
2 cloves garlic
¾ lbs. potatoes
4 carrots
1½ C. peas cooked, raw or frozen
1 C. turnips
1 T. butter
2 egg yolks, at room temperature
3 tomatoes (you can substitute with ½ C. tomato sauce or 2 T. tomato paste)
Thick cut bacon, about ¾ inch thick, cut unto cubes.

Peel and chop vegetables.

Saute the bacon with the onion. Do not let it brown.

Add 3 qts of water and the vegetables. Cook until the vegetables are done.

Beat the egg yolk. Let a cup of the broth cool down, stir in the yolks and add to the soup. Add the butter.

Serve with fresh baked bread.

Sopa De Tomate
Tomato Soup

6 large tomatos
1 large onion
2 large potatoes
1 T butter
1 cube Knorr boullian, beef flavor
Salt, pepper, oregano and cheese

Peel and cut potatoes into cubes.

Remove skin and seeds from tomatoes and cut into quarters.

Chop onion.

Add water to cover well. Cook until potato is soft.

Do not remove water. Puree and pass through the seive.

Add salt, pepper, knorr and butter. Stir and bring to a boil. Adjust for flavor.

If too thick, add a little milk.

Ladle into bowls and sprinkle with oregano and cheese of your choice. Serve with toast points.

Note: A can of tomatoes is a fine substitute.

Sopa De Agriã
Watercress Soup

½ C. chopped onion
3 T. butter
4 C. chopped fresh watercress leaves and stems
½ tsp. salt
3 T. all-purpose flour
1½ qts. chicken broth
2 egg yolks, lightly beaten
½ C. whipping cream

Saute onion in butter in a small pot over medium heat 5 minutes or until tender.

Stir in watercress and salt. Cover and cook 5 minutes or until leaves are wilted and tender.

Sprinkle flour over watercress. Cook 3 minutes stirring constantly. Stir in chicken broth. Simmer 5 minutes.

Place 1 to 2 C. of watercress mixture into blender. Process until smooth.

Transfer pureed mixture to a large saucepan. Repeat procedure with remaining watercress mixture.

Combine egg yolks and whipping cream in a small mixing bowl, mixing well. Gradually add 1 C. pureed watercress mixture, stirring constantly.

Gradually pour yolk mixture into remaining pureed watercress mixture, stirring well. Cook over low heat 2 minutes or until thoroughly heated. Serve warm or cold.

Sweets

Sweets do a lot for a lot of people. They do for me!

Growing up in the Azores, sweets were not eaten during the week. During the week, we did have a kind of cookie called biscoites that was a sort of a not-too-sweet cross between a cookie and a biscuit and was eaten with coffee or tea.

Weekend desserts were greatly looked forward to and as you will see in the following recipes, lemon is a big favorite of mine!

Bolo De Pero Apple Cake

First layer cake batter.
6 oz. or ¾ C. of flour
3 oz. or ⅓ C. sugar
4 oz. or ½ C. of butter
3 oz or ⅓ C. milk
2 eggs
½ tsp. baking powder
Juice of one lemon

8 inch round or brownie pan

Lots of apples peeled and sliced into wedges. Turn apple pieces in lemon juice and fill the pan.

For the crumb:
7½ oz. flour
4½ oz. butter
3 oz. sugar
1 tsp. cinnamon or more to taste
Pam (butter flavor)

Mix all the ingredients by hand.

Beat flour, sugar, butter, milk, eggs and baking powder. Spray pan wih Pam, butter flavor add the cake batter, all the apples and the crumb topping.

Bake at 350° for 60 minutes or until the apples are soft. Use a spring form pan.

Note: Use a cookie sheet under the cake pan. It's easier to wash a pan than clean the oven.

Bolo de Bananas
Banana Cake

½ C. butter
1 C. sugar
2 eggs
1 tsp. baking soda
4 T. sour cream
2 C. banana pulp, mashed
1½ C. cake flour
¼ tsp. salt
1 tsp. vanilla

Preheat oven to 350°.

Cream butter and sugar. Add eggs very lightly beaten add the soda, disolved in sour cream.

Beat well, then add the bananas, flour, salt and vanilla. Mix well.

Bake in well greased and floured 8 inch square or 9 inch tube pan for 45-60 minutes.

If you don't have the cake flour not a problem.

For each cup of flour, remove 1 T. and replace it with one tablespoon of corn starch.

Bolo De Fruta
Citrus Cake

1¼ C. flour
¾ tsp. baking powder
½ tsp. baking soda
½ C. unsalted butter
2 eggs
¾ C. powdered sugar
½ C. heavy cream
2 sweet limes, 2 oranges, 2 lemons
½ C. granulated sugar for syrup.

Take juice from all the fruits. Keep zest and slice citrus peels aside.

In a bowl, beat butter, sugar and zest until fluffy.

Add egg in the mixture one at a time and beat well.

Fold in combined dry ingredients and milk in batches.

Pour the batter in a parchment lined loaf pan. Bake 25 minutes in 350° preheated oven.

For syrup, boil sugar, juice and citrus peel until sugar disolves. Strain the syrup.

Once the cake is ready and warm, poke the cake with fork and pur the syrup over cake into the holes.

Allow cake to absorb the syrup and serve.

Bolo De Café
Coffee Cake

Batter:
1 C. sugar
1 stick of butter
2 eggs
2 C. flour
1 tsp. baking powder
1 tsp. baking soda.
1 tsp. salt
1 C. milk with ½ tsp. instant coffee grounds.

For Topping:
½ C. sugar
½ C. nuts (may leave out)
1 tsp. cinnamon (to taste)

Stir all together. Mix all the ingredients together.

Pour ½ of batter in the pan.

Sprinkle ½ topping then the rest of batter and top with the rest of topping.

Bake at 350° for 45 minutes in greased floured tube pan.

Bolo De Café
Citrus Spice Coffee Cake

1 pkg. dry yeast
½ C. sugar, divided
¼ C. warm water
½ C. butter softened
1 tsp. salt
2 eggs, beaten
1 C. milk
1 T. lemon juice
¼ tsp. ground nutmeg
4½ C. all-purpose flour

Dissolve yeast and 1 tsp. sugar in warm water, stirring well.

Let stand 5 minutes or until bubbly.

Cream butter and add remaining sugar. Gradually add salt, beating until light and fluffy.

Add eggs, milk, lemon juice and nutmeg. Beat well.

Stir in yeast mixture. Add flour, beat until smooth.

Turn dough out onto a floured surface and knead 5 minutes.

Place in a greased bowl, turning to grease top.

Let rise in a warm place, 85°, free from drafts, 2 hours or until doubled in bulk.

Punch dough down. Turn out onto a lightly floured surface Divide dough in half. Roll each portion into 1-inch diameter ropes.

Shape each rope into a loose coil in 2 greased 9 inch round cake pans, beginning at outer edge of pan. Firmly pinch ends to seal.

Spread half of topping over each cake.

Cover and repeat rising procedure 45 minutes or until doubled in bulk. Bake at 350° for 30 minutes or until golden brown.

Place on wire racks to cool.

While cakes are warm, drizzle with glaze or topping

Yield: 2 9 inch cakes.

Topping:
⅔ C. sifted powdered sugar
¼ C. butter
2 T. honey
1 egg white

Combine all ingredients, stirring until smooth. Yield about ¾ C.

Glaze:
2 C. sifted powdered sugar
3 T. boiling water
1 tsp. vanilla extract

Combine all ingredients and beat until smooth. Yield 1 C.

Bolo De Café
Coffee Cake with Coffee

1½ C. sugar (reserve 4 T.)
½ C. oil
¾ C. buttermilk
2 large eggs
1 T. vanilla
2 C. flour
½ tsp. salt
½ tsp. baking soda
1 tsp. baking powder
1 tsp. cinnamon
1 tsp instant coffee

Mix cinnamon and 4 T. sugar. Set aside.

In a bowl, mix together oil, milk and sugar. Add eggs and vanilla.

Combine dry ingredients into liquid ingredients and stir until smooth.

Pour half the batter in the pan and sprinkle cinnamon mixture and cover with the rest of the batter again.

Preheat the oven to 350°. Bake for 35 minutes or until done when inserted toothpick comes out clean.

Coffee Cake with Nuts

½ C shortening
¾ C. sugar
1 tsp. vanilla
3 eggs
2 C. sifted flour
1 tsp. baking soda
1 tsp. baking powder
1 C. sour cream
6 T. butter, softened
2 tsp. cinnamon
1 C. firmly packed brown sugar
1 C. chopped nuts (can exclude nuts)

Grease a 10 inch tube pan or 9x9x2 inch pan.

Cream shortening and sugar until light. Add vanilla. Beat in eggs, one at a time.

Sift flour, baking powder and baking soda

Add to the creamed shortening mixture alterately with the sour cream. Place half of batter into pan.

Combine the softened butter with the brown sugar, cinnamon and nuts. Sprinkle the batter with about half the mixture.

Add the remaining batter to pan and top with the rest of the brown sugar mixture.

Bake in preheated 350° degree oven, 50-60 minutes. Cool cake in pan for about 10 minutes before removing cake from pan.

Note: If you use the 9x9 pan, watch cake as it will not take as long to bake in a tube pan.

Bolinhos
Little Cakes

1½ C. flour
1 C. sugar
pinch of salt
1 tsp. vanilla
2 eggs
2 egg yolks
1 tsp sherry (may omit)
1½ C. dried currants
4 oz. Butter at room temperature

Whisk salt, flour and sugar separately.

In another bowl, beat butter and vanilla. Add egg yolks and sherry. Beat well.

Fold in flour and currants gently.

In greased molds, place batter half full and bake 15-20 minutes.

Note: I bake the little cakes in a madeline pan, but it also can be baked in a cupcake pan.

If the batter seemed to be a bit thicker, add a little more milk or water.

Bolo De Homen Pobre
The Poor Man's Cake

2 C. flour
1 C. sugar
½ C. cocoa, unsweetened
1 tsp. baking soda
½ tsp. salt
⅔ C. oil
1½ tsp. vinegar
1½ tsp. vanilla
1/2 C. cold water

Into a greased 9x13 inch baking dish, pour all dry ingredients. Pour wet ingredients into dry and mix with a fork until integrated.

Bake at 350° for 30 minutes or until a tooth pick inserted into cake comes out clean.

Pão De Lo
Pound Cake

10 eggs
1 C. sugar
2 C. flour
1 tsp. baking powder
½ tsp. salt
zest of one lemon

Preheat oven to 350°. Bake 30-35 minutes.

Beat eggs for 20 minutes and add sugar gradually. Gently fold in all the ingredients. Bake in a greased loaf pan.

Bolo De Limão
Lemon Bundt Cake

4 eggs
1 C. sugar
1 C. milk
⅔ C. seed oil (or vegetable oil)
1½ C. flour
zest of one lemon
1 tsp. baking powder

In a mixing bowl, add eggs and sugar and beat well.

Gradually add in oil and mix. Add milk, and dry ingredients. When blended, add lemon and blend well until mixture becomes smooth.

Pour into a greased, floured bundt pan. Bake at 350° for 30-40 minutes.

Lemon Cake

12 T. all-purpose flour
1 tsp. baking powder.
10 T. sugar
2 eggs
zest of 1 lemon
2 T. lemon juice
10 T. oil
10 T. milk
3 T. powdered sugar for dusting

Beat eggs and sugar until fluffy. Add juice, oil, milk and zest into the mixture.

Add combined dry ingredients in the mixture.

Pour the batter into greased loaf pan.

Bake for 40 minutes in 350° oven. Dust sugar on cake.

Bolo De Larange Con Azeite
Olive Oil Orange Cake

4-5 oranges
3½ cups all-purpose flour
1½ tsp. baking powder.
1¾ tsp. Kosher salt
5 eggs
3 C. granulated sugar
1½ C. light virgin olive oil
Powdered sugar for sprinkling

Grate the zest of 3 oranges and squeeze the juice at least 1½ C.

Mix flour, salt and baking powder in a bowl. Beat eggs and gradually add sugar in it.

Add flour and oil in the mixture. Add orange juice and zest to batter.

Pour the batter into a greased pan and bake 50 minutes at 350°. Once ready, serve or save for later. Bake in spring form or bundt pan. Watch oven if using bundt as it takes less time.

Bolo De Laranger
Orange Cake

1 C. sugar
4 oz butter
2 C. all-purpose flour
2 oranges juice
½ C. milk or orange juice
1 C. raison sultanas

Preheat the oven to 350° and bake for 40 minutes.

Beat sugar and butter until creamy. Add eggs and beat well.

Mix sifted flour, egg mixture, orange juice, or milk and raisins, in large bowl.

Pour into greased and floured bundt pan.

Once ready and cooled, serve cake with whipped cream.

The cake may be served warm or cold.

Bolo De Inverno
Winter Cake

1 C. unsalted butter
1 C. granulated sugar
2 eggs
1 tsp. vanilla extract
2 C. all-purpose flour
1 tsp. cocoa powder
1 tsp. each ground cardamon, cloves, cinnamon
1 tsp. baking soda
2 tsp. baking powder
1½ C. milk

Beat butter and sugar until fluffy. Next, you need to add eggs and vanilla extract. Beat well.

Whisk all the combined dry ingredients into the mixture.

Pour the batter in a greased cake pan.

Bake 50 minutes at 350° in greased floured loaf pan. When done, let it cool. Slice and serve.

Cabeceiras De Aniz
Anise Pillows

4 C. all purpose flour
1 C. sugar
1 C. butter
3 large eggs
5 tsp. baking powder.
½ tsp. salt
1½ tsp. anise extract

In a large bowl, mix all ingredients with a blender or mix by hand.

Shape a heaping tsp. of dough into 1½ inch half-moon shape. Place on a cookie sheet 1 inch apart.

Bake at 350° for 10-12 minutes.

I like rolling the dough in sugar before baking. I add a few drops of anise to the sugar first.

Makes about 5 dozen. Keeps well for 2-3 weeks.

We always made these cookies at Christmas.

Dream Cookies

1½ C. all-purpose flour
½ cocoa Hershey's Special dark
½ tsp. baking soda
½ tsp. cinnamon
½ t sp. salt
½ C. sugar
½ C. brown sugar
¼ C. smooth peanut butter
½ C. one stick unsalted butter at room temp.
1 tsp. pure vanilla extract
1 egg
2 T. strong brewed coffee cooled
1 C. peanut butter chips
½ C. butterscotch chips.

In a bowl, whisk the flour, cocoa, baking soda and salt set aside.

In the bowl of your stand mixer, fitted with a paddle attachments, beat together both sugar butter and peanut butter until light and fluffy about 5 minutes on medium speed.

Scrape down the sides of the bowl.

Add the vanilla, egg and coffee. Beat until well blended. Add the flour mixture and beat on low speed until just combined. Stop beating when streaks of white flour disappeared. Blend in chips

Scoop out rounded tablespoon of dough for each cookie. Using the bottom of a glass, flatten cookies about ½ inch thick. Dip glass in sugar or spray with Pam to prevnt sticking.

Bake 7 minutes. If you prefer crisp cookies, bake for 10 minutes.

Allow cookies ot rest on baking sheet 8 minutes before removing.

Bolachas Da Avó
Grandmother's Cookies

2½ C. sugar
8 C. flour
8 oz. butter
6 eggs
5 tsp. of baking powder

Mix all ingredients until smooth adding one egg at a time.

Roll cookies in sugar - cookie size about that of a walnut.

Bake at 350° for 15 minutes or until very lightly brown.

In our family, we call these cookies "everyday cookies." Not very sweet. If we stayed up late at night, we had a cup of tea and cookies.

This recipe makes a lot of cookies. Sometimes we made the cookies with grandmother. She'd take some home and we kept the rest.

Bolachas Da Avó
Grandmother's Nut Cookies

¾ C. sugar
6 T. butter
1 egg yolk
1 tsp. vanilla
1¾ C. all-purpose flour
½ tsp. baking soda
½ tsp. salt
1 egg white
½ finely chopped walnuts
¼ C. butter milk

In a mixing bowl, cream together sugar and butter. Beat in egg yolk and vanilla.

Stir togther flour, baking soda and salt. Add to cream mixture alternately with butter milk. Beat till smooth.

Drop dough by teaspoonfuls onto a cookie sheet covered with parchment paper.

Flatten cookies with the botom of a glass dipped in sugar.

Beat egg whites till frothy. Brush over cookies. Sprinkle with nuts.

Bake in 350° oven 8-10 minutes.

Buttermilk substitute: To make ¼ C. butter milk, place 1 tsp. lemon juice in a measuring cup and add milk to make ¼ C.

Lemon Cookies

1 (16.5 oz.) pkg. lemon cake mixture
1 (8 oz.) container frozen whipped topping thawed
1 large egg lightly beaten
1 C. powdered sugar

In a large bowl combine cake mix, whipped topping, one egg and mix well.

Shape dough into balls using a teaspoon of dough for each cookie.

Roll in powdered sugar and place on baking sheet lined with parchment paper.

Bake 10-13 minutes in a 350° oven. Let cool slightly. Remove cookies to a wire rack to cool completely.

I must confess that I love anything lemon. When I found this short cut to lemon cookies, I tried it. It's not too good to be true. It is truly good!

Good thing my mother or grandmother will never know.

Balachas De Limão
Lemon Sugar Cookies

Cookies:
2 large eggs
⅔ C. vegetable oil
2 C. all-purpose flour
2 tsp. baking powder
¾ C. sugar
2 tsp lemon zest (grated skin of lemon avoiding white area)

Beat at medium speed, eggs and oil. Mix until blended. Combine flour, baking powder and sugar. Add to the mixture all other ingredients and mix well.

Roll dough into a ball 1 tsp. at a time.

Bake at 350° for 8-10 minutes. Let cool on a wire rack.

Icing:
2½ C. powdered sugar
1 T. butter melted
2 T. lemon juice
1 T. water if needed
½ tsp. vanilla
1-2 drops yellow food coloring

Combine all ingrediendts. Stir until smooth. If needed add the water. Spread on cool cookies.

These cookies are good without icing also. It is my mother's recipe and my personal favorite cookie.

Mother's Basic Cookie Recipe

2 C. all-purpose flour
¾ C. sugar
½ tsp. baking powder
½ tsp. Salt
8 oz. Butter (1 stick)
2 eggs
1 tsp. vanilla

Basic because you can use 8 oz. of any dried fruit you like to the cookie dough.

Sift flour. Mix all ingredients until mixture is well mixed.

Add your favorite fruit and mix again.

Roll into a walnut size. Roll dough into raw white sugar.

Bake at 375° for 10-12 minutes. Adjust time to your oven.

Note: Refrigerate the dough for about ½ to 1 hour. Makes it easier to roll.

Olhos de Sogra
Mother-In-Law's Eyes

3 beaten egg yolks
1 (14 oz.) can sweetened condensed milk (Eagle Brand)
1 tsp. finely grated lemon peel
2 T. lemon juice
1 (12 oz.) bag pitted prunes.
Sifted powdered sugar

In a small saucepan, stir together egg yolks, condensed milk, and lemon peel. Cook over low heat, stirring constantly about 15 minutes or until mixture is thick.

Cool. Using a pastry bag with tube, fill prunes.

Roll filled prunes in powdered sugar and set in individual paper candy holders to store covered in refrigerator.

Makes about 4 dozen

We made these at Christmas time.

Malassadas Doughnuts

½ C. whole milk or water
2 T. unsalted butter
¾ tsp. kosher salt
2¼ tsp. yeast
½ C. sugar
3 large eggs
3½ C. all-purpose flour plus more for the work surface
Nonstick cooking spray
¾ C. granulated sugar

In a medium saucepan, heat milk, salt and butter on medium heat stirring frequently until it begins to form bubbles around the edges, about 5 minutes.

Remove from heat and let it cool until lukewarm.

In a stand mixer fitted with paddle attachment, add sugar and eggs, beat on medium high until thick, about 5 minutes.

Switch to dough hook, add milk mixture, flour, and yeast. Mix on low spead for 7 minutes. Add more flour if needed.

The dough should be just slightly tacky, but not sticky. Turn dough onto a lightly floured work surface, shape into a ball and place in a lightly buttered large bowl.

Cover with plastic wrap and let rise in a warm draft free spot until double in size, about 2-3 hours.

In a deep skillet or pot, add 1 inch vegetable oil. Heat to 350-375°. Wait! Dip your fingers in water. Pinch a piece of dough. Stretch into a round shape about 3-4 inches. Drop into the oil. When it is golden brown, flip over and cook the other side.

Have a cookie sheet with paper towels to absorb the extra fat from the malassadas.

In a plate with sugar, dredge malassada into sugar until coated.

We never used cinnamon in the sugar. Others do. You choose what you like better.

Malassadas are traditionly served at Carnaval time. I believe if you enjoy malassada, eat it anytime of year.

Note: Don't make the malassada too thick. It becomes a little bread like. When you stretch the dough, if it breaks into a hole it's okay.

Nuvens
Floating Clouds

1 qt. milk
4 eggs
1 C. sugar
1 tsp. cornstarch
1 tsp. vanilla
½ tsp. salt

Heat the milk on the stove and heat to nearly the boiling point.

Whip whites of eggs to a stiff froth and drop them by spoonfulls into the hot milk for a few minutes to cook

With a skimmer, remove these clouds to a plate.

Beat the yolks of the eggs with sugar, salt and cornstarch.

Stir into the milk until it boils.

Flavor if desired with lemon, orange, lime, raspberry and cool. Turn into a glass dish and lay the clouds on top of the custard.

Serve cold.

My mother called these clouds. Others called the same recipe Floating Islands.

Arroz Doçe

2 cups of water
1½ cups of milk
1 C. rice
1 C. sugar
6 egg yolks
1 lemon rind
1 T. butter
Salt and cinnamon

Add water, rice, salt and butter. Cook covered until water has evaporated, 20 minutes or so. Mix sugar with egg yolks, well mixed. Set aside.

Add the milk to rice. Stir often while cooking at low heat. When it reaches a creamy consistancy, remove from the heat, add egg and sugar mixture.

Serve in individual bowls or on one large platter. Sprinkle with cinnamon.

Note: the rice should be very soft. If the rice is a bit al dente, add more milk and continue cooking on very low heat. It can burn easily.

Butters and Cheeses

Butter Up

Pair one of these flavored butters with a loaf of homemade bread for a cozy treat on a cold winter day.

All these combinations go well with bread, but you have options, so treat your taste buds to one of life's little luxuries, the creamy goodness of buter from a crock.

Blue Cheese Butter

½ C. butter
¼ C. crumbled blue cheese

Combine. Serve with crackers as an hors doeuvre or on baked potatoes or steaks.

Chili Butter

½ C. butter
1 T. chili powder
1 tsp. ground cumin
½ tsp. ground red pepper

Combine. Serve on warm tortillas or rice.

Roll any flavored butter in wax paper and freeze it in a zip lock plastic freezer bag. It will keep well.

Chipolte Pepper Butter

1 tsp. chipolte peppers in Adobo sauce

Combine with ½ C. softened butter.

Serve on rice, baked potatoes, chicken or pork chops.

Citrus Butter

½ C. butter, softened
1 T. grated lemon rind
1 T. grated orange rind

Mix together. Serve on any seafood, chicken or pasta.

Herb Butter

2 T. chopped fresh dill
1 T. chopped fresh parsley
½ C. butter softened

Stir ingredients. Cover and chill 8 hours. Serve on assorted steamed vegetables, fish or chicken.

Honey Butter

2 T. honey
1 tsp. grated lemon rind
½ C. softened buttered

Combine. Serve on sweet potatoes, waffles, winter squash.

Lemon Anchovy Butter

½ C. butter softened
2 tsp. Anchoby paste
1 tsp. lemon rind

Blend together. Serve on seafood.

Lemon Herb Butter

½ C. softened butter
2 tsp. lemon zest
1 tsp. fresh chives
1 tsp chopped fresh oregano
1 tsp. hopped fresh parsley

Stir together. Yield: ½ C.

Lemon Pepper Butter

½ C. buter at room temperature
1 tsp. lemon rind
1 tsp. lemon juice

Blend together. Serve on steak, fish, chicken or shrimp.

Mediterranean Butter

3 T. minced pitted Kalamata olives
1 garlic clove, minced
2 T. basil oil
½ C. butter softened

Combine and serve on sliced French bread for an easy appetizer or on pasta, fish or chicken.

Pecan Butter

½ C. butter softened
⅓ C. finely chopped pecans, toasted
1 T. sugar

Mix together. Serve on pancakes, sweet potatoes, winter squash or gingerbread.

Shrimp Butter

10 oz. Steamed shrimp
1 T. minced onion
3 T. lemon juice
4 T. mayonaise
1½ stick of butter
8 oz cream cheese
1 T. horseradish
salt and pepper to taste.

Chop shrimp very fine. Add all ingredients and with a hand beater, beat until well blended .

Will keep in the fridge for a month. Freezes well. Great on toast or on tea sandwiches.

Walnut Honey Butter

½ C. softened butter
2 T. honey
¼ C. finely chopped walnuts

Heat oven to 350°. In a pan, place one layer of walnuts. Bake 5-7 minutes or until lightly toasted, stirring halfway through.

Cool 15 minutes. Add to butter, honey and walnuts, stir until it is well mixed. Yield about ¾ C.

Seafood Butter

2 tsp. Grated onion
1½ tsp. Old Bay seasonings
½ C. softened butter.

Combine well. Serve on any seafood or on baked potatoes.

Cheese

In all the Islands, cheese is produced. Some are co-ops, others are small independent artisans. The goat milk cheese usually is made and consumed fresh within a few days.

The cheese comes in different stages, some soft, semi hard and hard in colors from white to dark yellow.

Each Island's cheese has a difference in taste and texture.

The most famous cheese is Queijo de São George, (cheese from São George Island). They export to Portugal, U.S. and Canada.

At home, we made fresh cheese at least one a week. In Sao Miguel, most restaurants serve this fresh soft cheese with calda da pimenta with bread while you wait for your meal.

Boursin Cheese Spread

2 (16 oz. pkg.) cream cheese
1 (8 oz.) carton whipped butter (or whip your own with a little water added to butter)
2 cloves of garlic, pressed
¾ tsp. dried oregano
¾ tsp. basil
¾ tsp. thyme
¾ tsp. Pepper

Beat cream cheese at medium speed until smooth. Add butter and remaining ingredients. Mix until blended. Keep in the fridge for a month. Freezes well.

Great on a Kaiser roll with smoked salmon. Also makes great tea sandwiches. Note: Freezes well.

Queijo Fresco
Fresh Cheese

6-8 C. milk (warm)
1 T. salt
½ tsp. Renet (follow instructions on package)

Add renet and salt to milk and stir well. Cover with a tea towel and leave it on the counter 45-60 minutes.

When it is hard, break it and let it drain (whey) in the fridge. Line a colander with a napkin to drain. Also can use a cheese cloth. The one I had didn't work well. In 24 hours, it is ready to serve. We pour calda da pimento over the cheese. Serve with a French or Italian loaf of bread.

Note: I noticed that Lewes Dairy milk is better. It is a little creamier than others. It is my preference.

Salmon Cheese

1 tsp. minced onion
3 tsp. lemon juice
4 T. mayonnaise
1½ stick butter
8 oz. cream cheese, soft
1 T. horseradish
salt and pepper
smoked salmon or steamed to taste (can sustitute salmon for shrimp)

Beat all together at medium speed until smooth. Great on toast or French bread. Note: the cream cheese is a good substitute for a soft cheese we used.

Shrimp Paste

1½ lbs medium shrimp, cooked, peeled, and deveined.
¾ C. butter, softened
2 T. lemon juice
¼ tsp. onion juice
1½ tsp. salt
1¼ tsp. red pepper
¼ tsp. dry mustard
¼ tsp. ground mace (optional)

Position knife blade in food processor bowl. Place shrimp in bowl and cover with lid. Coarsely grind shrimp. A meat grinder may be used instead of food processor if desired. Combine ground shrimp and butter in a medium mixing bowl. Stir until well blended.

Add lemon juice, onion juice, salt, pepper, mustard and mace, (optional). Mix well. Refrigerate several hours. Serve on toast.

Tampanor

Chop:
2 tomatoes
1 cucumber (seedless)
1 red or white onion
1 can black beans (15.5 oz.)
1 can chick peas (15.5 oz.)

Dressing
½ C. olive oil and vegetable oil
½ C. to ⅓ C. vinegar
1 tsp. sugar
1 tsp. mustard, ground

Mix all together and stir dressing. Adjust to taste.

Add to vegetables. Stir and keep in the fridge at least 3 hours before serving. Overnight is best.

Note: It will keep for a week. If you don't have seedless cucumbers, simply remove seeds from the cucumber.

Tangy Sunday Night

Cream thoroughly equal parts of cream cheese and butter.

Add salt to taste, paprika and 1 tps. each, finely minced parsley capers, pickles, olives and green pepper.

If desired, flavor with anchovy paste.

You may use all ingredients or substitute with your favorites

Serve on freshly baked hard, crusty bread.

Potted Cheese

¼ lb. chedder cheese (grated)
2 T. butter
⅛ tsp. pepper
¼ C. heavy cream
yolk of one egg

Melt the butter. Add cheese and pepper. Add the cream to the beaten yolk. Pour into cheese mixture and cook, stirring constantly until thick and smooth. Pour into a jar and store in fridge.

My Sunday Memories
of Tangy Suppers and Butter Up Breads

My mother was one of seven siblings. Six lived with their families on the same small town.

On Sundays we had our main meal at noon, then every other Sunday afternoon, all six families, aunts, uncles, and cousins gathered at grandmother's house for cake, cookies, coffee and tea. It was a full house, 15-17 children at any one time and their parents.

Imagine the noise level! Different conversations going on, children running around squeeling.

It seemed that no one noticed. Some of the older cousins didn't come. They prefered to be with their friends.

As in any family, there is one troublemaker. Ours was no different. Most of the time, the girls disappeared upstairs to play with toys or games. The parents tried to send the boys out to the backyard to play ball.

One Sunday, the troublemaker sneaked up the stairs. We didn't like him, so we pushed him out the door. He laughed and locked us in the room!

We banged on the door to no avail. No one could hear us downstairs, so we just kept playing. One girl was in desperate need to use the bathroom.

I had the bright idea to give her a plastic bag that I found. She looked at the bag and said, "How?"

"Well when you gotta go, you gotta go. You figure it out."

She did. Now the question, what to do with the bag?

They all looked at me as I was called the problem solver. Of course, I came through one more time. I thought, "What a brilliant idea. Drop the bag out the window into the street." The problem was, the window was high and we couldn't see out to the street.

I dropped the bag out of the window. Luck would have it, at the same time, a farmer was passing by riding his horse. On the horse, he carried two milk cans from his saddle. Yes! He got a shower.

He was mad as a wet hornet, got off his horse and being a neighbor, he called grandmother and told her what happened.

That's when they found us locked in the room upstairs. Now we had all the adults standing in a semi-circle. No words were spoken, all eyes on us. I looked around to see all fingrs pointing at me.

Oh great, now all angry faces focused on me. I did the same thing. I didn't say a word.

I could tell my mother was trying to control herself. My father really got mad and in his normal calm manner said, "I will take care." He turned to me and said, "Did the cat get your tongue?"

"No, but I can chirp like a canary!" He loved canaries.

I knew one of his few rules was if it's funny, no punishment. He smiled, and I told the story, but not before I asked that the troublemaker must be present.

I could tell my father was thinking, "That's my girl," by the look he gave me.

The troublemaker's parents immediately took him home.

What happened? I am sure he got what he deserved.

I have fond memories of Sunday afternoons at grandmothers with all the cousins. We all got along. Well, most of the time!

The other Sundays, we went to my my other grandparents. My father was one of five children. Four lived in town, but only one of my uncles had chidren. They lived one house away, so the two girls came over all the time. The brothers were older and had girlfriends.

We played a lot of board games. My favorite was dominos and my uncle played with us for hours. I got pretty good.

It was different there. The noise came from guitar playing and singing. Neighbors and friends passing by would stop by and dancing would erupt into a party.

I loved being in both places for different reasons. By the time we got home, no one was very hungry.

These are some of the recipes my mother had prepared for Sunday nights suppers.

Teas, Flavorings, and Other Drinks

In the early days, tea was the drink. To be honest, the coffee was not very good. Tea bags were not used.

Our neighbor had tea plants up in the hills. I used to help pick the tea leaves with her. At the end of the day, she gave me a large basketful. She also taught me how to process the tea.

I learned to roll the leaves as if you knead bread on a board with the heel of your hand. The leaves break down, releasing some of he bitterness. Then the fermentation begins in a warm dark place.

I don't remember how long it takes. When it's done, the leaves and spread on wood trays to dry. The first pick of the season makes the best tea. We had excellent tea to last the year.

Winter Teas

Heat an earthen or china tea pot by rinsing it with boiling water.

Then, put in one tsp. tea or one tea bag for each cup of water.

Pour freshly boiled water directly on the tea leaves or tea bags and steep 3-5 minutes.

Serve with sugar, honey, milk or lemon if desired.

With lemon or orange, serve tea hot, allowing a slice of lemon or orange to each cup, adding a few cloves if desired.

Lemonade

Juice of one lemonade
1½ C. water
4 T. sugar

Add the sugar to lemon juice and water and stir until disolved. Add crushed ice if desired. Makes one large drink for a hot summer day.

With Flavored Sugar

Add to sugar, lemon rind or orange. Pack and store in jars to be used later to sweeten tea.

Wash rind of lemon or orange and wipe dry, then rub sugar on rind.

Also may use cloves or a stick of cinnamon and lemon peel to sugar and store in a glass jar.

Ginger Syrup

Pour 1 qt. of water over ½ C. ground ginger root.

Let stand for 48 hours. Pour off water into kettle, carefully leaving sediment undisturbed. Measure water add an equal amount of sugar, boil 10 minutes.

Pour into hot sterilized jars and seal.

Use as flavoring with tea or fruit juices.

With Preserved Fruits or Rum

Serve tea hot allowing 1 tsp. of rum, preserved fruit, strawberry, raspberry, cherry or pineapple preserves to each cup.

Pour the tea hrough a cheese cloth and serve.

Lemon or Orange Syrup

Grated rinds of 6 lemons
Juice of 12 lemons
2 qt. boiling water
1 lb. sugar
Add grated rind of lemons to juice and let stand overnight.

Pour water over sugar, stir until sugar is disolved. Boil 5 minutes. Cool. Add lemon juice. Bottle and seal. Serve with equal amout of water.

If you make orange syrup, add a little lemon with orange.

Makes 2 ½ qts.

Spiced Syrup

1 T. each, whole cloves, allspice, cinnamon
4 lbs. sugar
2 qts. water

Tie spices in a bag. Place sugar and water in kettle. Let boil 5 minutes or until clear. Add spices and cook until syrup is well flavored. Pour into hot sterilized bottles or jars and seal.

Use with fruit juices and flavoring drinks.

Makes 2 qts.

Chocolate Syrup

To make chocolate drinks:
2 C. of sugar
1 qt. Water
4 squares (4 oz.) unsweetened chocolate
½ tsp. salt
2 T. cornstarch
2 T. cold water
2 tsp. vanilla

Boil water and sugar 5 minutes. Add chocolate, salt and the cornstarch. Dissolve in cold water. Stir until smooth.

Cook 3 minutes. Cool, add vanilla, and store in a jar in a refrigerator.

Use 2 T. to a glass of milk when ready to serve. Note: Whipped cream or on ice cream is great.

Tips

A Few Short Cuts to Clean
and
Save Time and Money

A Fridge That Smells

We know that other foods can absorb smells.

There is a solution to control that strong onion flavor and still create great recipes.

Just before preparing your onion based recipe, cut the onion in slices and put in a mixing bowl with cold water and a little vinegar.
Wait about 20-30 minutes and then use the onions as always.

If your fridge smells bad, just add a bowl with vinegar or milk. Do not cover bowl. Leave over night or longer to absorb the smells and thus preserving your food.

Keep left over onion in a glass bowl with airtight lid in the fridge. Don't use plastic bowls.

Celery

Wrap celery in foil and keep in the vegetable drawer.

Honey

Honey does not need refrigeration.

Avocados

Leave avocados on the counter. When the avocado is ripe, the stem comes of easily and the skin is puckered.

Bananas

To keep bananas longer, use 2 blue absorbant pads for vegetables. Wrap the stems with clingfree plastic wrap. Keep the bananas and the blue pads in an airtight container.

Green Onions

Keep onions in a glass. Add ½ inch water just enough to covr the roots. Cut the tops as needed. Onions will keep growing. Keep on the counter.

Herbs

Mint, Basil and Parsley are great to have on hand. Wash the herbs. Let dry, chop and put in a zip lock bag. Keep in an airtight container in the freezer. Use as needed.

Asparagus

Keep in a bunch with the elastic around. Add 1 inch water in a glass. Cover with a plastic bag in the fridge.

Potatoes, Onions and Garlic:

Best to keep in a cool dark place.

Tomatoes

Keep tomatoes on the counter top, not in the fridge

Cheese

It's very simple to presrve from going dry. All you need to do is spread a very thin layer of butter on all sides of the cheese exposed to air. Keep in fridge.

Also, keep cheesewrapped in parchment paper in the fridge. Before serving cheese, bring the cheese to room temp.

Seeds

Seeds used in breads. Best to keep in air tight container in the fridge. Nuts as well.

Mushrooms

Mushrooms are best kept in a brown bag in the fridge to extend their life.

Basil, Mint, Parsley

Keep in a glass with 1 inch of water on the counter or in fridge.

Fruit

If the fruit you just bought seems un ripe, take a plastic bag and put the fruit you want to ripen together with an apple in the bag. This will accelerate the maturation of the fruit. Put the bag in the ridge. After a day your fruit will be ripe and ready to eat.

Citrus

To keep lemons or limes longer, in a bowl, add fruit and fresh cold water for 30 seconds. Then dry each piece of fruit well. Keep in a zip lock bag. Remove as much air as possible. Keep in the fridge for about 3 months.

Vinegar

We all know that vinegar is a good cleaner, but the smell is not too pleasant. When I use a lemon, I keep the peel cut into strips and add to the bottle of vinegar.

Brown Flour

Spread flour on a cookie sheet or pie plate. Put in a hot oven 325 and stir often. After it begins to brown, untie. It is all colored. Keep always on hand for coloring and thickening gravies. Keep in an air tight container for 3-6 months.

Soft Boil Eggs

When serving soft boiled eggs, your goal is yummy yolks and perfectly firm whites. Cook eggs in boiling water for exactly 7 minutes. Place in a bowl of ice water to cool completely before peeling. Eggs should be at room temp. before cooking.

Buttermilk Substitute

To make ¼ C. buttermilk, place 1 tsp. Lemon juice in measuring cup and add milk to make ¼ cup.

What to do if you don't have eggs for baking?

If you are out of eggs, replace with the same ounces of applesauce.

No Cake Flour?

If you don't have cake flour, not a problem! For each cup of flour, remove 1 T. of flour and replace with 1 T. cornstarch.

Whipping Cream

Need heavy whipping cream? Replace with milk added to with 30 % melted buter to make the same liquid ounces.

Need wine for cooking?

If a recipe requires wine, replace with chicken broth and 1/8th lemon.

The Lessons I've Learned

I've learned from my grandmother and my mother. While it may seem obvious, it didn't until much later.

They never took notice of huge accomplishments in their everday lives, but when I looked back over a period of time, I began to see things take a different shape.

They showed up everyday, and did good work. They stuck to the task at hand and carried on happily.

So I grew up with a sense that anything could be made. There were very few store bought items in my grandmothers or in our house.

The things that were purchased, were kept for a very long time, then updated and altered to serve other purposes.

Just as the cabinets were stocked with foods grown, harvested and cooked in the same manner, they believed you don't plan a menu, the ingredients you have, thats what you cook with.

From grandmother and mother I got the sense of my ability to shape the world around me, even if it's only one little corner.

While cooking, I find if I am out of one item, I simply substitute with another, making it my own.

As my grandmother and mother before me did, I too say, "I made do and it was good."

The lessons I've learned have served me well. For that I am grateful to be part of a family of two strong women whom I am priviledged to have known and loved.

By example, I learned the love of cooking and the strength of family.

I know they would enjoy my food.

My techniques are different as well as the flavors, but the soul carries on in the food I cook.

Last Words

All across the globe recipes are passed along to others to enjoy.

By doing so, it allows us to experiment with food and challenges us to be more creative.

Cooking doesn't need to be limited to diverse or mouth watering dishes, but the art of sharing good food with others is a work of love.

Hope you will enjoy cooking some of the recipes in this book and share the love.

M.R. Tiso

Recipe Index

Flat Breads:

Bolos De Leite / Flat Bread De Sao Miguel 14
Bolo De Sertão 15
Pão De Sertão (Tiso Style) 16
Pita Bread 17
Saboroso Pão / Savory Focaccia 18
Beer Bread 19
Pão De Milho / Corn Bread 20
Pão De Milho Leve / Corn Light Bread 21
Pão De Milho Fresco / Fresh Corn Bread 22
Pão De Milho Da Ilha / Island Cornbread 23
Pão De Mistura / Mixed Corn Bread 24
Pão De Milho Na Sertão / Old Fashioned Skillet Cornbread 25
Pão De Milho Especial / Special Cornbread 26

Yeast Breads:

Country Bread 28
Cheese Bread 29
Combination Bread 30
Dark Bread 31
Round Herb Loaf 32
Pao Caseiro / House Bread 33
Raison Bread Twist 34
Pao Rustico / Rustic Bread 35
Sour Dough 36
Rye Bread #1 37
Rye Bread #2 38
Rye Bread #3 39
Spicy Spiral Loaf 40
Basic White Bread 41
White Bread 42
White Bread (Sponge Method) 43
Coffee Sticks 44
Whole Wheat Bread #1 45
Whole Wheat Bread #2 46
Whole Wheat Bread #3 47
Whole Wheat Bread #4 48

Rolls:

Potato Rolls 50
Soft Rolls 51
Bow Knots 52
Braided Rolls 52
Clover Leaf Rolls 53
Cresent Rolls 53
Mound Rolls 54
House Rolls 54
Tea Rolls 55

Sweet Breads:

Pão Doce De Pero / Apple Bread 58
Pão De Banana / Banana Bread 59
Pão Doce De Cenoura / Carrot Bread 60
Cranberry Bread 61
Poppy Seed Bread 62
Prune Bread 63
Pão Doce De Abobora / Pumpkin Bread 64

Sweet Yeast Breads:

Massa Savada / Sweet Egg Bread 66
Massa Doce / Sweet Dough 67
Pão Doce Rico / Rich Sweet Bread 68
Pão Doce Rico / Rich Sweet Bread - Variation 69
Pão Doce Rico / Rich Sweet Bread – Variation #2 69
Pão Doce Rico / Rich Sweet Bread – Variation #3 70

Main Dishes – Beef:

Baked Beef Stew 74
Meatball Stew 75
Roast Beef 76
Rump Roast Beef 77
Carne Asada / Roast Beef 78

Main Dishes – Chicken:

Broiled Bacon Wrapped Chicken 82
Chicken a-la King 83

Chicken Pot Pie 84
Galinha Desfiada Com Legumes / Chicken Pot Pie 85
Cold Chicken and Pasta 86
Chicken Stew in Bread Bowls 87
Chicken Wellington 88
Conja De Galinha / Chicken Risotto 89
Conja de Rita 92
Rosemary Chicken and Brie 93
White Chili 94

Main Dishes – Fish:

Bocalhau con Batatos e Cebolas / Cod with Potatoes and Onions Cod Stew 96
Cod Stew 97
Bacalhau a Gomes De Sa / Salt Cod With Potatoes, Onions, and Black Olives 98
Creamed Salt Cod 100
Salt Cod With Potatoes 101
Rice With Fish 102
Island Baked Bass 103
Fish Cakes 104
Fried Fish with Sauce 105
Broiled Flounder with Mushroom-Wine Sauce 106
Flounder in the Bag 107
Poached Grouper 108
Grilled Salmon Steaks 109
Steamed Salmon 110
Baked Stuffed Red Snapper 111
Baked Snapper 112
Broiled Fillets of Trout 113
Grilled Trout 114
Trout with Almond Lemon Sauce 115
Pan Fried Seatrout 116
Albacora Grilhada / Grilled Fresh Tuna 117
Grilled Tuna Steaks 118
Oven Baked Tuna 119
Tuna Chowder 120
Crabmeat with Curried Rice 121
Broiled Lobster Tails 122

Creamed Lobster 123
Shrimp Pie 124
Shrimp Scampi (#1) 125
Shrimp Scampi (#2) 126

Main Dishes – Lamb:

Golden Lamb 128
Broiled Lamb Chops 129
Grilled Lamb Chops 130
Carne De Ovelha Asada / Lamb Pot Roast 131
Braised Lamb Shanks 132
Lamb Stew 133
Lemon Garlic Leg of Lamb 134
Roast Lamb and Herbs 135
Roasted Lamb Shoulder 136
Serrasco no Espeto / Shish Kabobs 137

Main Dishes – Pork:

Broiled Pork Chops 141
Cranberry Glazed Pork Chops 142
Pork Chops Supreme 143
Porco Rechiado / Pork Stuffed Eggplant 144
Marinated Pork Roast 145
Pork Roast 146
Pork Loin Roast 147
Bifes De Porco Con Ananas / Pineapple Pork Chops 148
Carne De Porco Asada / Roast Pork with Dressing 149

Main Dishes – Other Recipes:

Guisado De Favas con Chaurico / Sauteed Favas with Sausages 152
Macaroni and Cheese with Truffle Oil 153
Ervilhas Guisadas a Portuguesa / Peas Portuguese Style 154
Chaurico Con Ervilhas / Sausage and Peas 155
Carne Con Feijao E Vinho / Portuguese Chili 156
Chaurico Con Feijao E Arroz / Chaurico with Rice and Beans 157

Pancakes:

Panquecas / Plain Pancakes 160

Panquecas (#2) / Cornmeal Pancakes 161
Pancakes 162
Panquecas De Bananas / Spiced Banana Pancakes 163
Panquecas De Familia / Family Pancake Recipe 164
Panquecas De Mistura / Mix Pancakes 165
Overnight Sensation for Christmas Morning 166

Salads:

Salada / Salad 168
Salada (#2) 169
Salada De Repolho / Cabbage Salad 170
Chick Peas Vinagrette 171
Grao De Bico Com Couve / Chickpea and Kale Salad 172
Chick Pea and Rice Salad 174
Salada De Cove / Kale Salad 175

Condiments, Relishes, Glazes, Marinades, and Sauces:

Super Simple Vinaigrette 178
Molho De Tomate / My Grandmother's Ketchup 178
Homemade Mayonnaise 179
Mustard Sauce 179
Hot Sweet Mustard 180
Molho De Mostarda / Mustard Sauce 181
Calda De Pimentos or Pasta De Pimentos / Pepper Paste 182
Olives 183
Pimenta Moida / Pepper Relish 184
Cortume De Pimenta / Pickled Peppers 185
Pimenta Salgada / Salted Peppers 185
Relish De Pero / Applesauce Relish (short cut) 186
Cranberry Orange Chutney 186
Glaze 187
Cranberry Glaze 187
Apricot Glaze 188
Custard Glaze 188
Glaze for Lamb 189
Honey Glaze 189
Glaze for Tenderloin Pork 189
Vinha D'Alhos Marinade 190
Tangy Marinade 190

Marinade for Pork Tenderloin	191
Manteiga De Malho / Butter Sauce	191
Basic Brown Sauce	192
Malho Escuro / Brown Sauce	192
Brown Mushroom Sauce	193
Malho Picante / Hot Piquant Sauce	193
Caper Sauce	194
Capers Sauce	194
Café de Paris Sauce	195
Molho Para Filetes / Sauce for Thin Steaks	195
Horseradish Sauce	196
Horseradish Mustard Sauce	196
Horseradish and Sour Cream Sauce	196
Mushroom Sauce	197
Mushroom Cream Sauce	197
Mushroom Pan Gravy	198
Roast Pan Gravy	198
Rich Pan Gravy	199
Raison Sauce	199
Malho De Vinho / Wine Sauce	199
Molha De Vilao	200
Sweet and Sour Sauce	200
Lemon Sauce	201
Molho De Limao / Lemon Sauce	201
Brown Egg Sauce	202
Creamy Egg Sauce	202
Spiced Port Wine Sauce	203
Sour Cream and Chive Sauce	203
Remoulade Sauce	204
Molho De Sardinhas / Sardine Sauce	204
Sour Cream Tartar Sauce	205
Tartar Sauce	205
Snapper Sauce	206
Seafood Sauce	206
Dill and Mustard Sauce	207
Mint Sauce (#1)	208
Molho De Ortelao / Mint Sauce (#2)	208
Tangy Mint Sauce (#3)	208
Molho Branco / Basic White Sauce	209

Molho Branco / White Sauce 209
Medium White Sauce 210
Thick White Sauce 210
Cream Sauce 210
Cheese Sauce 211
White Gravy 211

Sides:

Glazed Fried Apples 214
Baked Fresh Asparagus 214
Wrapped Asparagus Spears 215
Toast Baskets 215
Asparagus with Mushrooms and Cream Sauce 216
Crème De Feijao / Bean Puree 217
Broccoli Baked with Cheese Sauce 218
Broccoli Parmesan 219
Fresh Brussels Sprouts 219
Carraway Fettucine 220
Carrot Fritters 221
Puree De Cenaura / Carrott Puree 222
Baked Cauliflower 222
Dumplings 223
Split Green Beans 224
Mushroom Casserole 225
Potato Pancakes 228
Molho Verde Com Batatas / Potatoes with Green Sauce 229
Pie De Batatas / Potato Pie 230
Pure De Batata Ricas / Mashed Potatoes for Company 231
Batatas Esmagadas / Smashed Potatoes 232
Repolho Vermelho / Red Cabbage 233
Sebola Vermelho Com Azeitonas / Red Onion and Olive Tart 234
Arroz Verde / Green Rice 235
Green Rice Casserole 236
Curried Rice 237
Breding / Stuffing 238
Ananas De Forno / Baked Pineapple 239
Apple Glazed Sweet Potatoes 240
Glazed Sweet Potatoes 241
Sweet Potatoes and Pineapple 242

Recheadas De Tomate / Tomatoes with Dressing 243
Arroz De Legumes / Vegetable Rice 244
Baked Zucchini Fans 245
Zesty Zucchini Saute 246

<u>Soups:</u>

Sopa Cove De Flor / Cauliflower Soup 248
Sopa De Castanhas / Cream of Chestnut Soup 249
Sopa De Galinha Con Milho / Chicken and Corn Soup 250
Crab Soup for Company 251
Sopa De Paixe / Fish Soup 252
Sope De Feijao Con Couve / Greens with Red Bean Soup 253
Caldo Verde / Green Soup 255
Acorda De Otrelao / Mint Soup 256
Mushroom and Barley Soup 257
Sopa Do Norte / Northern Soup 258
Outra Sopa De Batata / Cream of Potato and Leek Soup 259
Sopa De Batata / Potato Soup 260
Sopa De Abobara / Pumpkin Soup 261
Cream of Shrimp Soup 262
Shrimp Soup 263
Sopa De Verao / Summer Soup 264
Sopa Para O Jantar / One Dish Supper Soup 265
Tortelini Soup Stew 266
Sopa De Legumes / Vegetable Soup 267
Sopa De Tomate / Tomato Soup 268
Sopa De Agria / Watercress Soup 269

<u>Sweets:</u>

Bolo De Pero / Apple Cake 272
Bolo de Bananas / Banana Cake 273
Bolo De Fruta / Citrus Cake 274
Bolo De Café / Coffee Cake 275
Bolo De Café / Citrus Spice Coffee Cake 276
Bolo De Café / Coffee Cake with Coffee 278
Coffee Cake with Nuts 279
Bolinhos / Little Cakes 280
Bolo De Homen Pobre / The Poor Man's Cake 281
Pao De Lo / Pound Cake 282

Bolo De Limao / Lemon Bundt Cake 282
Lemon Cake 283
Bolo De Larange Con Azeite / Olive Oil Orange Cake 284
Bolo De Laranger / Orange Cake 285
Bolo De Inverno / Winter Cake 286
Cabeceiras De Aniz / Anise Pillows 287
Dream Cookies 288
Bolachas Da Avo / Grandmother's Cookies 289
Bolachas Da Avo / Grandmother's Nut Cookies 290
Lemon Cookies 291
Balachas De Limao / Lemon Sugar Cookies 292
Mother's Basic Cookie Recipe 293
Olhos de Sogra / Mother In Law's Eyes 294
Malassadas / Doughnuts 295
Nuvens / Floating Clouds 297
Arroz Doce 298

Butters and Cheeses:

Blue Cheese Butter 302
Chili Butter 302
Chipolte Pepper Butter 302
Citrus Butter 303
Herb Butter 303
Honey Butter 303
Lemon Anchovy Butter 304
Lemon Herb Butter 304
Lemon Pepper Butter 304
Mediterranean Butter 305
Pecan Butter 305
Shrimp Butter 305
Walnut Honey Butter 306
Seafood Butter 306
Boursin Cheese Spread 308
Queijo Fresco / Fresh Cheese 309
Salmon Cheese 309
Shrimp Paste 309
Tampanor 310
Tangy Sunday Night 311
Potted Cheese 311

Teas:

    Winter Teas 316
    Lemonade 316
    Flavored Sugar 316
    Ginger Syrup 317
    Lemon or Orange Syrup 317
    Spiced Syrup 318
    Chocolate Syrup 318

www.ingramcontent.com/pod-product-compliance
Lightning Source LLC
Chambersburg PA
CBHW061245230426
43662CB00021B/2438